The True Story of the Clarks (1837-1955)

The True Story of the Clarks (1837-1955)

A Cutlery Village Family

Elizabeth Anne Banas

ISBN: 1512194905
ISBN 13: 9781512194906

Elizabeth Anne Banas

The True Story of the Clarks (1837-1955)

A Cutlery Village Family

Edited by Andrienne G. Clark

For Geo-
My forever man

Table of Contents

Foreward

After reading Elizabeth Banas' *The True Story of the Clarks' of Bay State Village (1837-1955)*, I feel as though, I have finally been introduced to my husband's extended family. I met my future husband, John Paul Clark, whom everyone called Jack, on April 1957 when we were both in college. He attended American International College in Springfield, Massachusetts and I attended Clark University in Worcester, Massachusetts. We met at a crew race between AIC and Clark at Lake Quinsigamond in Worcester. Four years later in August 1961, we were married in my hometown of Claremont, New Hampshire.

During those four years I met very few of Jack's relatives, aside, of course, from his parents, John G. Clark and Ruth Miller Clark. I frequently heard Jack's parents refer to this brother or that aunt or cousin, but I don't recall meeting many of them or seeing them frequently. On the other hand, I did meet his mother's immediate relatives: her brother and his wife and their two children, and her sister. They lived in Springfield and Jack took me to visit them on several occasions, so by the time Jack and married, they were familiar to me.

Not so with names like Foran and Aunt Julia, and the Goodhinds. I did meet Margaret Foran several times, although I was never certain how she was related to the Clarks. After our marriage, I saw Nellie and Walter Dobler fairly often because they came to the

Clarks for Thanksgiving several times, and I came to know them fairly well. Yet my knowledge of Jack's extended family was always rather sketchy. The passage of time has dimmed my recollections of them as well. This is why I have so enjoyed reading *The True Story of the Clarks of Bay State Village (1837-1955)*. Elizabeth's book is a sensitively written, honest, and well-documented account of the lives of first-generation immigrants Hannah Madigan Conners Clark and her husband John Clark and their descendants in Northampton and surrounding areas. She presents a vivid picture of the challenges, struggles, hardships, sorrows and joys they faced over a period of three generations. For the Clarks each new setback was an obstacle to be overcome by hard work, persistence and faith.

While the Clarks are one particular family, their experiences are not unique. Most Irish immigrants, as well as other ethnic groups and their children faced years of hardship as they struggled to establish a foothold in the United States and achieve the American dream. This is why Elizabeth's book is a great contribution to our history. The story of one family shows how much we all have in common. It is why this book will be of interest, not only to members of the Clark family, but to anyone who wants to know more about our nation's history, who enjoys reading biographies, or who simply likes "a good read."

Andrienne G. Clark

Acknowledgements

I would like to begin by thanking Andrienne Clark for editing this book and her tireless dedication to preserving the Clark family history through the John G. Clark Collection at the W.E.B. Du Bois Library.

Family members, many of whom I have never met in person, have also contributed to this project. I would like to thank: James Bills, Margaret Donaghey, John Ennis, Joseph Gilboy, Edward Murch, David McElroy, Helen Myers, Cathleen Smith, Janet Richer (1930-2014) and Margaret Walz for sharing their research, photographs from their personal collections and their knowledge of the Clark family.

Three family members, who contributed to this book passed away during the research phase of this project: Anne (Cleary) Goodhind (1932-2012), Peg (Cleary) Leitl (1918-2010) and Edward V. Cleary (1935-2014). Their contributions were unique in that they knew many of the individuals I have written about in this narrative.

I would like to express my gratitude to fellow genealogist and historian Tina Peters, who assisted me in my research in Shelburne Falls and Buckland, Massachusetts.

I would like to thank Suzanne and Stephanie Smith, the current owners of the former (James) Clark family residence for allowing Geo to photograph the property for the book.

I would also like to thank Elise Bernier-Feeley, local history and genealogy librarian at Forbes Library, who kindly shared her knowledge of local Catholic history with me.

I would like to express my deepest appreciation to the W.E.B. Du Bois Library, Special Collections at UMASS Amherst, the *Boston Herald, Springfield Republican* and the *Daily Hampshire Gazette.*

Last but not least, I would like to thank my husband Geo who has stood by me throughout this project. He spent many hours and days driving to research locations. He has photographed sites and scanned hundreds of documents for this book. Without his support, this project would not have come to fruition.

Introduction

John Clark and Hannah Madigan were my maternal great-great grandparents. Shortly after their marriage in 1866, John obtained employment in a cutlery in Greenfield, Massachusetts and thus began the long history of the Clarks in the manufacturing of silverware.

While the cutlery industry provided John and Hannah with a means to support their family and attain home ownership, the culture of the manufacturing village created challenges and hardships for subsequent generations.

Most of John and Hannah's children and grandchildren never experienced financial success during their lifetime. War, the Depression and personal tragedies continually beset this family. However, their fortitude and faith in God allowed them to continue to move forward.

There will be Clark descendants who will dispute my findings. I would like all of my readers to know that I have persevered to present a clear and accurate account of the history of this family. I have performed exhaustive searches in public records and documented the facts contained in this narrative. Stories told by family members which I have woven into the text are rooted in personal knowledge. The writings of John P. Clark (1930-1988) pertaining to the character and history of this family are echoes of stories told by family members and experiences from my own childhood. Many readers will find this book to be a fresh perspective on what they already know or have been told.

When in doubt about the veracity of a story, I did not include it in this account.

That being said, it is my pleasure to introduce you to the Clarks.

Elizabeth Anne Banas
Clark Descendant

I

John Clark and Hannah Madigan

John Clark and Hannah Madigan were my maternal great-great-grandparents. It became clear to me over the many years I researched the Clark branch of my family that no one in the last three generations knew very much about them.

Despite my best efforts, I have discovered very little about John Clark. His naturalization record states that he was born on 16 May 1837 in Liverpool, England.[1] According to the data entered into the record, he immigrated to New Orleans at the age of thirteen on 2 December 1850.[2] Beyond this information and the data contained in his marriage record little else is known about his origins.

The number of individuals who bear the name "John Clark" and are possible matches for this ancestor are staggering. The fact that he did not use a middle name or initial, decreases the probability of locating him through reliable resources. What little insight I have into his life, came to me by way of public documents created in the United States, interviews with Clark descendants and a draft of a narrative history written by a cousin I never had the opportunity to meet.

A red spiral bound notebook containing a compilation of personal anecdotes and a draft of a narrative history of the family entitled, *The Clark Chronicles* was found among the personal items of the late John (Jack) Paul Clark (1930-1988), great-grandson of John Clark (1837-1902).[3] Jack wrote:

John Clark, according to Clark family tradition, had shipped out of Liverpool England in 1861 as a seaman and jumped ship in Charleston, South Carolina. The story goes that he enlisted in the Confederate Army and after a brief period of service made his way to Deerfield probably around 1862. John was probably an Englishman but he married an Irish girl and his son, my grandfather James M. Clark was half Irish.[4]

It is likely the tradition regarding John Clark's military service was passed down to Jack through his father State Representative John G. Clark (1902-1972) and while some of Jack's information is inconsistent with John Clark's statements in public documents, I believe the truth about his origins, his military service and his migration to Massachusetts, lies somewhere in this tradition.

There are other stories, which corroborate Jack's information. One such story is an account given by John Clark's grandson Leo Clark to his daughter Cathleen (Clark) Smith. Cathleen stated that when Leo was a young boy he overheard his grandfather talking to a neighbor about his service in the Confederacy.[5]

Yet another tradition, shared by John Ennis, John Clark's third great-grandson, states that he was drafted into military service during the Civil War. The story further asserts that he later "jumped ship," to marry Hannah.[6] This tradition implies that John had a relationship with Hannah prior to or during his service. This would place him in Massachusetts before the war.

Additionally, John Clark's second great-grandson, James Bills passed on an unidentified photo of a young sailor attired in a Civil War naval uniform to me.[7] The young man in the photo bears a strong resemblance to John Clark's grandson, William C. Clark and his third great-grandson Jesse Sampson. The provenance of the photo is unknown.

Collectively, the stories, the photo and public records are interesting bits of information that may help solve the mysteries surrounding John Clark's origins and his military service.

However, more evidence is needed to support a conclusion consistent with family traditions and the identity of the unknown subject in the photo.

Even though little is known about John Clark, there is a persistent rumor, which has traveled throughout the family, concerning a pair of pistols with ivory handles, which ostensibly belonged to him. This narrative states that Mae (Clark) Cleary was in possession of the pistols and while attending William Clark's wake in April 1961, she stated she planned to give the guns to William's sons because they were the only ones left who carried the Clark name.[8]

I lived with my grandmother Mae on and off when I was a young child. I also lived next door to her for many years. I never heard her speak of the pistols, nor did I ever see any guns in her home. Early in the nineteen-seventies, my parents (Anne and Albert Goodhind) moved into Mae's home to care for her in her old age. When Mae died, all of her worldly possessions remained in the house. To the best of my knowledge, there were no pistols among the items she left.

James Bills has had a lifelong relationship with the men and he has stated that he has no knowledge of the pistols. [9]

If the guns exist, it is likely they are in the possession of another branch of the family or were sold long ago.

While unanswered questions and rumors regarding John Clark abound, information entered in both his marriage record and naturalization record indicate that he was born in Liverpool, England on 16 May 1837 to Hugh Clark and Mary Carroll.[10]

Hannah is an enigmatic character as well. I have followed her through public records and still so many questions about her life remain unanswered. How I wish she could speak to me. Only she could explain the disappearance of her first husband from her life and the inconsistencies in the records. She is, by far, one of the most complex people I have researched in my career as a genealogist.

Hannah's given name, surname (Hannorah Madigan), and birthplace are etched in the timeworn Clark headstone at St. Mary's Cemetery in Northampton, Massachusetts. There it is stated that she was born in Robertstown, County Limerick, Ireland. This data is not in accord with the Irish records, which state she was born in Shanagolden, County Limerick.

In 1989, Madigan descendant Helen Myers, commissioned a search of birth, death and marriage records at the Limerick Archives. A report of the findings, signed by Chris O'Mahoney, manager and research officer at the archives notes that Hannah was born 23 October 1826.[11] The report also states that the "Madigan family came from the parish of Shanagolden."[12]

In 2011, I contacted author and Madigan researcher, Father Dan Madigan for additional evidence to support Chris O'Mahoney's data. Father Madigan, who was born and raised in Shanagolden, has viewed the Irish parish records. He confirmed that 23 October 1826 is the birth date entered for Hannah in the register book for the parish of Shanagolden.[13]

I did not conduct research to determine how Father Dan may be connected to my branch of the family. He is the author of *The Ramblings of Father Dan Madigan.*

On my last trip to Ireland, I visited both Shanagolden and Robertstown. It is noteworthy that the parishes are contiguous.

While the information on the headstone sheds doubt on Hannah's origins, the evidence strongly suggests that Shanagolden was her birthplace.

Hannah was born to Daniel and Catherine Madigan.[14] Although her given name was Hannorah, once in the United States, she identified herself as Hannah.

Hannah grew up with two siblings: John born 11 January 1831[15] and Ann, born 30 March 1825.[16]

The O'Mahoney report names Daniel Madigan and Catherine Wallace as Ann's parents. However, her name is recorded in the Massachusetts state death register as Ann (Wallace) Myers.[17] Her mother is entered in the register as Catherine Dullard and her father as Patrick Wallace. It would appear that Ann was the product of a former marriage between her mother and Patrick Wallace. However, the marriage records in County Limerick do not commence until after Catherine's marriage to Daniel Madigan and consequently a former marriage (Dullard-Wallace) cannot be confirmed.

Ann's daughter, Annie (Myers) Egan, created a scrapbook in which she pasted newspaper articles, marriage and death notices over the pages of an old book. Vital statistics are scribbled in the margins and across blank pages. The entries and clippings include all of the Madigan kin and their major life events. Extended family members and friends are represented within the pages of the scrapbook, as well.

One of Annie's entries states that Catherine Wallace "Madigan" died in 1859 at the age of seventy-six.[18] She also noted on the same page: "Ann Madigan married to Patrick Myers, November 5, 1852."[19] Transcribed data and information passed down from older family members are often the least reliable sources. Nonetheless, Annie's reference to her mother as "Ann Madigan" is yet another conflicting statement, which casts doubt upon the identity of Ann's biological father. Since marriage records are not available for that period, questions pertaining to Ann's biological father and whether or not Catherine's surname was Dullard remain unanswered.

To date, I have not located a passenger list or documentation to confirm when Hannah and Ann arrived in the United States. There is no evidence that John emigrated. What is known is that Ann married Patrick Myers on 3 November 1852 in Greenfield, Massachusetts.[20]

Little more than a month later, Hannah married Michael O'Connor on 10 December 1852.[21] While the surname entered in the marriage index was O'Connor, I found alternate and abbreviated forms of the name (Connors/Conners) substituted in subsequent public records. The most common abbreviated form of the surname is Conners. For the sake of consistency, I will refer to the O'Connor/Connors/Conners surname as Conners throughout this narrative.

The 1855 Massachusetts state census found Hannah and Michael living in Cheapside Village, a rough section of Deerfield, located on the outskirts of Greenfield.[22] Cheapside was comprised of a collection of small homes and tenements. During this period the village had an increasing population of immigrants from Germany, Holland and Ireland, who were employed by the local factories.

According to census records, Michael was employed as a cutler, probably at the John Russell Cutlery.[23] John Russell Cutlery was the largest employer in the area. It was also an unhealthy, unsafe, working environment. Along with work related accidents, cutlery workers often developed lung disease. Diseases of the bronchi were prevalent among cutlery employees, due to inhalation of metal particles and dust expelled from the machinery into the air. Many cutlery workers met an untimely death due to their occupation.

While working conditions for the men employed by John Russell Cutlery were dangerous, living conditions in Cheapside were unhealthy, at best.

Old Calvary Cemetery, which is located just outside of the parameters of Cheapside, is the resting place for scores of Irish immigrant workers and their families. Many are interred in unmarked graves. The headstones bearing the names of infants and children who met an untimely end bear witness to the torrent of disease that permeated the factory village in the early and mid-nineteenth century.

Hannah experienced her share of death and suffering in Cheapside. Between 1853 and 1860, she gave birth to five male children. Three of them passed before the age of three. John, born 8 September 1853,[24] died on 8 August 1854 of unspecified causes.[25] Less than two months later, on 25 September 1854, Hannah gave birth to another son, named Michael Junior.[26] This child succumbed to measles on 17 October 1856, at the age of one year, eleven months.[27] A third child, named Daniel, was born on 9 June 1856.[28] He passed on 16 November 1856, at the age of five months, due to water on the brain.[29]

Two subsequent children, William born 24 October 1858[30] and Thomas born 18 April 1860, [31] survived well into adulthood.

What occurred in the Conners family between 1860 and 1865 is unknown. The 1865 Massachusetts state census found Hannah residing in a tenement in Greenfield under her maiden name with her two surviving sons.[32] The entry notes she was "single" rather than widowed.

There is no evidence by way of public records to indicate Michael Conners died between the 1860 federal census taking and the 1865 Massachusetts state census. His death was not reported to the town of Deerfield, nor is there a record for his death in nearby Greenfield.

I have searched the register books in both towns and I have noted more than a half-dozen entries for Michael Conners/O'Connor and other alternative spellings of the surname, who passed between 1860 and 1865. The statistics I have collected pertaining to his age, do not match the entries in the registers. Since the children's deaths were reported, it is likely, though not conclusive evidence, that something else occurred.

While Annie (Myers) Egan's scrapbook contains entries and data for the Myers, the Clarks and the extended family, Michael Conners [O'Connor] name is conspicuously absent.[33] This led me to question if, indeed, his death was the cause of his absence from the 1865 census. Even though it did not seem likely, given that Hannah was a Roman Catholic, I requested a search of divorce records held by the Massachusetts Supreme Judicial Court. The courts response stated they had nothing on file.

Since Hannah remarried, it is reasonable to conclude that Michael died. However, there is no evidence in public records to support this conclusion. Whatever the cause of Hannah's circumstances after 1860, she was not on her own for very long.

II

A New Marriage: A New Life

It is likely that John and Hannah met in Greenfield, Massachusetts. The earliest record of John's residency can be found in the information filed at the Northampton City Clerk's office in January 1867 by F.I. Lynch, the clergyman, who performed the Conners-Clark marriage.[34] A certified copy of the record states the couple was married on 22 December 1866 in Northampton.[35] Biographical information entered in the certificate indicates that both Hannah and John resided in Greenfield. John's entry states that he was a twenty-eight year-old laborer, born in Liverpool, England to Hugh Clark and Mary —.[36] The certificate also notes that both parents were born in Ireland and that it was John's first marriage. Hannah's entry states that it was her second marriage and that she was thirty-one-years-old.[37] Her father's surname was recorded sans his forename (Daniel).[38] The age noted in Hannah's entry is clearly in conflict with her birth record in Ireland, which states that she was born in 1826. Her age based on the records supplied by both Chris O'Mahoney of the Limerick Archives and Father Dan Madigan, indicate that she was forty years old at the time of the marriage.[39] Inconsistencies in her birth date, as well as her birth data noted in census records and other public documents, are ubiquitous.

Hannah and John were pronounced husband wife before God, by Father Lynch at St. John the Baptist, Roman Catholic Church on the corner of Church and King Street in Northampton. Saint John the Baptist was the first Roman Catholic church in Northampton. The building was erected in 1844 and served the Roman Catholic population in the surrounding areas as well as Northampton. St. John's was torn down circa 1881. Agnes Fox Playground was built on the site where the church once stood.[40]

On 23 June 1868, Hannah gave birth to twins, a boy and a girl, whom they named James[41] and Mary R. [H.].[42] The following year she gave birth to another female child born 11 November 1869, whom they named Jane.[43]

By then, the family had moved back to the Cheapside section of Deerfield, as the children's births are recorded there.[44]

While little is known about the Clarks during this period, the 1870 federal census provides some insight pertaining to the socio-economic challenges this young family faced. According to the enumeration data, the Clarks were likely living in close proximity to the cutlery that employed both John Clark and his eleven-year-old stepson William Connors.[45] A survey of the neighborhood showed that nearly all of the residents were employed as cutlers. Most families resided in tenements. Indeed, John and Hannah resided in a three-family dwelling. It is impossible to determine from such limited information the condition of the dwelling. However, accounts I have read depict Cheapside as an overcrowded community that lacked decent sanitation. The survey also indicated that most residents in the neighborhood were immigrants.

There were no grand homes employing servants in Cheapside, though there were women employed as domestic servants living in rented housing in the village. Undoubtedly, this family was struggling economically. [46]

In 1870, John Russell Manufacturing moved to nearby Turners Falls. This event was the cause of much suffering in Cheapside, where most families were living on a limited income. Rents in Turners Falls were higher than most cutlers could afford and many families were left with no means of support. This event may have precipitated the Clarks' removal to the hilltown of Buckland in 1871.[47]

Buckland was the home of Lamson & Goodnow, a cutlery known for the production of fine silver. L & G's claim to fame was a set of silver flatware the company produced and presented to President Ulysses Grant after the Civil War ended.

The company was expanding and increasing its workforce during the years after the war and with the growth came an increase in the population of both Buckland and the town of the Shelburne Falls, located on the opposite side of the Deerfield River.

The Clarks settled in a plain, recently-built house on Elm Street, a short walk from the cutlery. I was able to determine through deed research that they purchased the property from Ann Murphy.[48] Unfortunately, the deed for the transfer of the property was not on file and consequently, I was not able to determine the sale date.

Bits of information can be gleaned from public documents and census records regarding the family and their life during the Buckland years. It was by serendipity that I happened upon an obscure newspaper item pertaining to John Clark, dated 14 June 1875:

> Last Fri. John Clark, John Kramer, Jack Costello and Tom Morrisey, were arrested by Sheriff Swan and Constable White for drunkenness and disorderly conduct, and lodged in the lock up. Before bed time Tom was let out, and before morning Kramer and Costello, with outside help, let themselves out through the grates of the window and have run away. Sat. morning before Samuel D. Bardwell, Esq., Morrisey was discharged, and the sentence in the case of Clark was suspended.[49]

John Clark filed naturalization papers in 1876. His Primary Declaration provides the best genealogical information we have regarding his origins. The declaration filed in Franklin County

Supreme Judicial Court in Greenfield states that he was born in Liverpool, England on 16 May 1837.[50] The document further states that he was thirteen years old when he arrived in New Orleans on 2 December 1850 and notes that he had lived in Buckland for five years.[51] Sherriff Swan, who arrested him the preceding year and Samuel Bardwell, the local magistrate, who heard his case, were his witnesses at the proceedings.[52]

Clearly the move from Deerfield to Buckland was a move up for the family. Buckland was a cleaner, less congested and healthier community to raise a family. Moreover, it would appear the family had gained some financial stability with the purchase of a home. Still on 22 September 1879, John and Hannah sold their Elm Street house to George Crittenden, a local lumber dealer, for two hundred dollars.[53]

While the sale of the Elm Street property from the Clarks' to George Crittenden was signed, sealed and delivered, there were obviously misgivings on the part of John and Hannah. The very day of the transfer, another transfer between the Clarks and George Crittenden was executed which conveyed the property back to Hannah Clark for two hundred thirty-five dollars; thirty-five dollars more than Crittenden paid for the property earlier in the day![54] The sale price indicated that the Clarks believed they made a mistake in selling the house. It is noteworthy that John Clark did not partake in this matter.

Hannah eventually sold the Elm Street house on 16 Dec 1882 for a whopping four hundred dollars[55] to Christian Adler, an employee of the German Harmonica Company in Shelburne Falls.[56] The Clarks back peddling upon selling the house in 1879 rewarded them with a financial windfall three years later.

The family relocated to Northampton just as a major change was underway at Clement Manufacturing, a cutlery located in Bay State Village. W.W. Lee or Billy Lee, as he was known to the employees of the shop, became a partner in the company in 1882.[57] Under his direction business increased and with the growth, the company expanded.[58] By then John was experienced in the table cutlery trade and that is where he found employment. Eventually, James and the Connors brothers worked there, as well.

It is unknown where the Clarks found housing upon their arrival in Northampton. However, in February 1883, Hannah purchased a home.[59] The wood frame colonial, which is still standing, is located on Riverside Drive. The sale price was $1250.[60] The deed contained a reference to an $800 mortgage given by the Northampton Institution for Savings.[61] John did not hold title to the property with Hannah. In their relationship, Hannah apparently was the partner in charge of the family finances. She managed the money well. She was able to sell the Buckland property for a mighty profit and with that money, she purchased a larger home with a sizeable down payment of $450. With the help an inflation calculator, I was able to determine that $450 in 1882 was equivalent to $10,227.27 in 2013.[62] Given that most manufacturing workers and their families lived in company housing or tenements during this period, due to a lack of resources, this was quite remarkable.

III

Hopeful Beginnings and Sad Farewells

The Clark children were young teenagers when the family moved into the house on Main Street (Riverside Drive) in Bay State Village.[63] It was a convenient location, within walking distance of the cutlery and a short jaunt from the village school. Their elder half-brothers, both in their early twenties by then, were living nearby at different addresses. According to the city directory, Thomas was employed as a clerk at E.E. Hart.[64] William worked in a paper factory.[65] However, the city directory for 1887-1888 listed both men's employment as Clement Manufacturing and their address as Main St, Bay State.[66]

Today Northampton is known as a cultural Mecca. However, when the Clarks relocated to the Bay State Village section of the city, Northampton was still essentially a mill town, fueled by the silk industry and smaller manufactories like Billy Lee's cutlery shop. However, when compared to the hilltowns of Buckland and Shelburne Falls, Northampton was a sophisticated and exciting city. The center consisted of an array of shops, churches and a courthouse. The nearby neighborhoods of Round Hill and Elm Street were comprised of large, magnificent homes and the newly formed Smith College, also located on Elm Street, was not far from the village.

While exposure to diverse segments of society can be educational and inspiring, how this family fit into the community and whether they were inspired or defeated by the environment of the small mill village tucked away from the flow of the city are questions that would be answered as the Clark children entered adulthood.

Mary, known as "Mamie," married Edward J. Beckett on 17th November 1886 at St. Mary's Church in Northampton.[67] The *Northampton Daily Herald* reported: "The marriage of Edward Beckett and Mamie Clark on the 17th last, was an important social event in our midst and congratulations are flying thick and fast in the vicinity of this estimable couple."[68]

The newspaper article, which portrayed a young couple celebrating a joyful event, belied the fact that Mamie was pregnant when she walked down the aisle of St. Mary's Church to take her vows. Little more than four and a half months later, a female child whom they named Kate was born in April 1887.[69] Her birth date was recorded in the state birth register for the City of Northampton as 15 April 1887.[70] However, according to the death register, her death came on 6 April 1887 at 2 days old.[71] It can be assumed she was born on 4 April 1887.[72] The cause of death was listed as "premature." [73]

Nearly everything I have compiled pertaining to Mamie and Edward has been gleaned from public records, census returns and newspaper items. Mamie, like Hannah and John, is something of an enigmatic character in so far as there are no stories pertaining to her, and much to my chagrin, I have been unable to locate a photograph of her.

One of the most interesting facts I discovered in the course of my research is that both Edward and Mamie were twins. I found this extraordinary.

Edward[74] and his twin, John,[75] were born in Northampton on 17 June 1862 to Thomas and Esther (Moore) Beckett. Their father was an Irish immigrant employed as a laborer.[76] Six children preceded the twins and with the addition of a child born in 1864, the number of siblings swelled to nine.[77] Certainly, this family experienced economic difficulties. Beyond this information, I have no knowledge of Edward Beckett's origins and his early childhood.

According to the information entered in the state marriage register for the City of Northampton, Edward was employed as a cutler at the time of the marriage. It is likely he knew the Clarks vis-à-vis his employment.

Mamie, like many local women, worked in a silk mill.[78] The silk mills were an economic bastion in Northampton and the surrounding villages. Companies like Corticelli employed primarily females. Often, the wages earned by the women in a family brought prosperity and stability to the household. It is unknown whether Mamie continued to work after Kate's death.

By 1888, Mamie was pregnant for the second time. She gave birth to a male child named George on 15 February 1889.[79] The infant succumbed approximately one month later on 19 March 1889 from "exhaustion."[80] This medical term is non-specific. It is defined as a slow or prolonged death.

A third child, named Edward was born to the Becketts on 16 November 1891.[81] He was followed by Annie born 10 March 1894[82] and James I. born 23 August 1896.[83]

During the first decade of their marriage, Mamie and Edward were always on the move. They relocated eight times between 1887 and 1898.[84] However, they remained within the City of Northampton. I have been told that less affluent families, who lived in rental properties, moved frequently in order to take advantage of cheaper rents. An alternative explanation for their numerous relocations may have been their ever-expanding family.

Sometime in 1897, Mamie and Edward Beckett relocated to Providence, Rhode Island.[85] Census records show that subsequent to the family's relocation from Northampton to Providence, Edward was employed in a jewelry shop as a polisher and later as a janitor.[86]

The Beckett family continued to grow with the births of Raymond Clark Beckett born on 6 Aug 1899;[87] Jane Ester born 21 Apr 1901;[88] died on 8 December 1901 of "convulsions;[89] Florence Agnes born 27 March 1904;[90] Mary Gertrude born 18 February 1906;[91] Ruth H.

born 7 September 1910[92] and finally Helen Irene born 2 September 1913.[93] Helen died on 2 September 1913 of "duodenal indigestion" and "convulsions."[94]

There was no respite from tragedy for Edward and Mamie. Incredibly their eight year old son James, drowned while playing with a "plank in a pond." on 14 June 1904.[95] He was the fifth of Edward and Mamie's eleven children to die.

Births, deaths and tragedies notwithstanding, the family was still on the move. A sampling from city directories showed the Becketts relocated twelve times between 1901 and 1924.[96]

While Mamie was struggling with losses and raising a brood of children, her twin brother James was following a different path

IV

Jimmy Clark: Athlete, Husband and Father

I have no way of knowing when Jimmy discovered he could run faster and jump higher than most mortals. The earliest newspaper article I was able to locate pertaining to his athletic career ran in the 2 August 1886 edition of the *Springfield Republican*, where it was reported that while competing in games sponsored by the Caledonian Club in Southwick, Massachusetts, he broke his arm in two places.[97]

Jimmy celebrated his 18th birthday in June, two months prior to the competition in Southwick that left him with fractured arm, but it is likely he was participating in competitions much earlier.

A subsequent article, which appeared a little over a year later on 29 August 1887 reported: "About five hundred people joined the picnic of Hibernians at Mt. Tom grove Saturday. In the athletic sports James Clark won first prizes of $3 in the hop, step and jump, running high jump and 100 yards dash."[98]

Sometime in the late eighteen-eighties, Jimmy joined the fire department in Bay State. It was through this association that he became a member of the W.A. Bailey Racing Team. The team was named in honor of a former fire chief. Research of newspaper items and historical accounts did not provide any information pertaining to when the team was organized.

Athletic teams created from fire department personnel were common in this period. The venue for competitions were musters. Musters often opened with a parade of fire fighters in full regalia. It was a carnival-like atmosphere with food and other forms of entertainment. The events were held all over New England and across the United States. Interestingly, firemen contests were the first organized athletic competitions in the United States. The contests were so popular, international exhibits of the games were held in Paris as early as 1867.[99] An international Fire Congress was also held there in 1900, as part of the International Exposition and Olympic Games.[100] I have been told that Jimmy participated in the Olympics in the early part of the 20th century. This morsel of information may have been a reference to the Fire Congress in Paris that was part of the Olympic Games. However, I was unable to locate any evidence to support this claim. Certainly, a competition in Paris that included local firemen would have been reported by the press.

Jimmy quickly became a recognizable athlete through his participation with the W.A. Bailey racers in competitions throughout New England. Eventually, he competed in national contests, as well. A tongue-in-cheek news article published in the *Springfield Republican* on 6 October 1890 is an allusion to his popularity among the local sports fans: "Several hundred people were at the fair-grounds Saturday afternoon to see the 100-yard race between James Clark and P.H. Garvey of the Lynch Company of Holyoke. Garvey was given two yards start and won by about a foot."[101]

The Bailey hose runners' reputation earned them the title of "W.A. Bailey's World's Champion Hose Running Team."[102]

Undoubtedly, the promise of prize money was always a strong incentive for Jimmy to compete, but prize money was not a substitute for a steady pay check and he continued to work alongside his father and brothers at Billy Lee's cutlery in Bay State. To the best of my knowledge, he never worked in any other establishment.

Just as Jimmy's star was rising, his life changed dramatically. According to my grandmother Mae (Clark) Cleary, Jimmy caught a glimpse of his future wife, Mary Ann Cashman in a store in Northampton. Mae did not have any knowledge of the details of their courtship. [103]

Jimmy and Mary Ann did not live far from one another. The Cashmans resided on Nonotuck Street near the silk mills.[104] The Clark residence was just a few miles away.

We know from the wedding portrait that Mary Ann was attractive. Mae told me she had auburn hair and like Jimmy's mother, she was an Irish immigrant. Beyond that, she was a stylish woman who loved clothes.

Mary Ann was born c. 27 September 1869 in County Cork, Ireland to Cornelius Cashman and Bridget McGrath.[105] Cornelius was a farm laborer and prior to their marriage, Bridget was a servant in Rathcormac.[106] Mary Ann had seven known siblings: Ellen (Helen) born 30 August 1866;[107] Julia born 11 November 1870;[108] Margaret (Maud) born 22 June 1873;[109] Daniel born 11 July 1875;[110] Roger born 6 July 1877,[111] Catherine (date of birth unknown)[112] and William (date of birth unknown).[113]

The Cashmans did not put down roots for very long. The children's birth records indicate they were born in seven different townlands. However, for the most part, the family lived in townlands in the vicinity of Cork City. Lodging was included as part of a farm laborer's wages and so wherever Cornelius found work is where the family lived.

Mary Ann's eldest sister Helen (Ellen) immigrated ahead of the family, arriving in the Port of New York on 30 May 1881.[114] The rest of the family followed on 18 September 1882.[115] Peg Leitl told me that the family first settled in Beckett, Massachusetts. Unfortunately, there are no records to confirm that statement.

When the Cashmans arrived in Northampton, Mary Ann, who was a young teenager, obtained employment in a silk mill. It would appear she led an unsettled and difficult life.

Jimmy and Mary Ann shared much in common by way of their Irish ethnicity, religion and their occupations in local industries. However, they were very different spirits. Cousin Jack Clark wrote: "Jimmy was an outstanding person, generous and friendly. Mary Ann seems to have had a less admirable streak in her."[116] This characterization was repeated throughout my research.

Jimmy and Mary Ann were married by Father Charles McManus on Tuesday, 26 February 1895 at the Church of the Annunciation in Florence.[117] A wedding announcement appeared the following day in the Daily Hampshire Gazette: "The ceremony was performed by Rev. Father McManus, before a number of friends. The bridesmaid was Miss Julia Cashman, sister of the bride, and her dress as well as the bride's was of light tan brocade. Mr. Tom Keneavy of the center acted as best man. A reception followed at the home of the bride."[118]

Tom Keneavy was Jimmy's friend and a fellow member of the W.A. Bailey Running Team.[119]

The wedding portrait depicts a slender, fragile bride with a narrow waist. Amazingly, Mary Ann was five months pregnant at the time.

Jimmy and Mary Ann settled into an apartment on Federal Street in Bay State and on 29 June 1895, Mary Ann gave birth to a baby boy whom they named Leo Earnest.[120] Four subsequent children were born in the next decade: Mary Hannah born 24 May 1897,[121] ostensibly named after Jimmy's twin sister Mary Beckett; Helen (Nellie) born 11 September 1899;[122] John George (Jack) born February 1902;[123] Joseph born 4 April 1904, died the same day[124] and William Cornelius born 22 December 1905.[125]

Upon Jimmy's marriage to Mary Ann, the large home Hannah purchased for the family in 1882 was nearly empty. Four of their five children were living at other addresses. Jane known as "Jennie," then twenty-five years old, was the lone sibling left in the elder Clark's household. There had been many changes in the family in little more than a decade. Before year's end, life for the Clarks' would change forever.

Members of the W.A. Bailey Running Team. Jimmy Clark is seated on the right. Reproduction courtesy of W.E.B. Du Bois Library, Special Collections and University Archives, University of Massachusetts-Amherst.

The Cashman-Clark wedding party. Standing: Julia Cashman
and Tom Keneavey. Seated: Jimmy and Mary Ann.

V

Resolution, Roses and Bereavement

A death in a family is always a shock, even when it is inevitable. I am sure the Clark's were stunned when Hannah passed of heart disease on 4 May 1895.[126] A notification of her death appeared in the *Daily Hampshire Gazette* the following day:

> "Her many friends were pained to hear of the death of Mrs. John Clark this morning, after a short illness due to heart trouble. Mrs. Clark has been in poor health for some time, yet the end was hardly realized to be so near. The deceased has won many warm friends during her long residence here and the entire community tenders their sincerest sympathy to the bereaved family."[127]

Hannah's wake was held at her home on Riverside Drive in Bay State. A brief item ran in the 7 May 1895 edition of the Daily *Hampshire Gazette*, which noted: "Mrs. John Clark's funeral was largely attended from her late residence Monday morning."[128]

Since the Clarks were Roman Catholic, it is likely there was a funeral mass at the Church of the Annunciation in Florence, followed by a committal service at St. Mary's Cemetery on Elm Street.

Hannah's age is misstated in nearly all public documents, so it is no surprise her death certificate incorrectly stated that she was fifty-eight years old, when in fact she was sixty-eight.[129]

No one is alive to attest to the circumstances among Clark kin at the time of Hannah's death. However, I found the transfer of the Clark home to daughter Jane shortly after Hannah's death surprising. An explanation regarding the transfer can be found in the third line of the deed. It is John's voice in this matter.

> I, John Clark of Northampton in the County of Hampshire and Commonwealth of Massachusetts, in consideration of One Dollar and other valuable consideration, paid by Jane E. Clark, my daughter of said Northampton, who has lived with and assisted in supporting us, the receipt whereof is hereby acknowledged, do hereby remise, release and forever quitclaim unto the said Jane E. Clark...all my right in and title to all that real estate in the City of Northampton of which my wife died seized..."

> To have and to hold the granted premises, with all the privileges and appurtenances thereto belonging to the said Jane E. Clark and her heirs and assigns to their own use and behoof forever. Except the homestead right which by law I have in said property.[130]

The transfer of title was recorded at the Hampshire County Registry of Deeds on 16 May 1895.[131] The deed was executed just twelve days after Hannah died. It was a deed in vain. John never held title to the house. He claimed title via a Homestead Declaration filed 16 March 1883.[132]

However, there is no question that Hannah held title to the house in her name alone and while John may have owned interest in the house by way of intestate succession laws, he was not the sole heir. Since Hannah died without a will, all of Hannah's children held interest in the property, as well. The deed was signed, sealed, delivered and acknowledged, but the transfer was not legally binding.

I do not know what transpired in the years following Hannah's death, however another deed dated 8 June 1897, provided a resolution to the problematic transfer of the Clark home in 1895.

On the afternoon of 8 June 1897, the Clark family gathered in the presence of Attorney John O'Donnell for the probation of Hannah's estate and the sale of the family home. John O'Donnell was the same attorney who drew up the deed for the transfer of the property from John Clark to daughter Jane (Jennie) shortly after Hannah's death. According to the deed, the buyers Thomas and Alice Halpin of Northampton paid "One dollar and other consideration," for the house.[133] There was an outstanding mortgage on the property, which the buyers agreed to pay.

John Clark, William Connors, Thomas Connors, James Clark, Mary Beckett and Jane (Jennie), witnessed and signed the deed.[134]

The legal description of the property, which ended with the following sentence, clarified who held interest (ownership) in the house: "These premises we inherit from Hannah Clark our mother."[135]

It is unlikely family members knew about the prior transfer of the property.

It is unclear where Jane and John lived upon the sale of the property.

Just months after Hannah's estate was settled, her sister, Ann Myers died unexpectedly on 16 September 1897.[136] Ann was preparing to move to a new address, where carpeting was about to be installed.[137] The cause of death was noted in the state register as organic heart disease.[138] Ann was the Clark siblings' only known aunt. Her death was reported by the *Northampton Daily Herald*:

Mrs. Anne [sic] Myers died at the home of her son on Bright Avenue yesterday after a short illness from heart trouble. Mrs. Myers has been a resident of this city for the past six years coming from Turners Falls, where she lived many years. During her residence here she has made many friends by her

kindly disposition, being a woman of true Christian character and a devoted member of St. Mary's Church...[139]

Ann left behind three adult children: Michael,[140] Margaret[141] and
Anna Maria, known as Annie.[142]

A fourth child named Catherine died 2 August 1854.[143]

Ann also gave birth to a stillborn infant in Gill, Massachusetts
on 15 June 1863.[144]

Ann had been without her husband for many years. Patrick
Myers died in 1869 from a lung condition (consumption) associated
with his work in a paper mill in Montague.[145] He is interred in Old
Calvary Cemetery in Greenfield. However, there is a memorial in
remembrance of him etched in the headstone on the site where Ann
was laid to rest in St. Mary's Cemetery in Northampton. It was her
wish to have his name included on the stone.

Ann's death occurred just as Jane was preparing for her approaching marriage to Timothy McCarthy. I have limited knowledge of the McCarthy family. However, according to public records,
Timothy[146] and his twin sister Mary[147] were born 18 November 1870 to
Patrick McCarthy and Johanna (Hannah) Twohey of Northampton,
Massachusetts.[148] Both parents were born in Ireland. Patrick was a
laborer at the time of Timothy's birth.

Five subsequent children followed the births of Timothy and
Mary: Catherine, John, Eugene, Anna, and Patrick Jr.[149]

By the time Timothy married Jane (Jennie), his father, Patrick
was a coal dealer.[150]

The 27 October 1897 edition of the *Springfield Republican* reported the McCarthy-Clark wedding:

Miss Jennie E. Clark of Bay State and Timothy F. McCarthy
of King Street were married at St. Mary's Church this afternoon at 4:30, the ceremony being performed by Rev. John
Kenny. The bridesmaid was Miss May E. Dorsey of Bay

State and the best man was John J. McCarthy, brother of the groom. The couple proceeded to the alter while the strains of the Lohengrin wedding march were being played by Miss Minnie Kiely. The gown worn by the bride was of cream colored silk with pearl and lace trimmings and she carried bride roses...

This evening a reception will be given at the home of the groom's father, Patrick McCarthy on King Street. There have been over 350 invitations sent out and the house will be filled with the numerous friends of the popular young couple. The 1840-1911company will include guests from New Haven, Hartford, Springfield, Holyoke and Ware. Beckmann will cater. Both of the contracting parties are well known in this city and have hosts of friends. The bride has been employed in the dining room at the Norwood hotel, where she has been most efficient and a favorite with the guests. The groom is the son of Patrick McCarthy, the well known coal dealer and is in the plumbing business with Cutting & Mack...[151]

Four children were born from this union: John Patrick born 19 May 1899;[152] Anna born 6 January 1902;[153] Timothy J. born 25 April 1905[154] and Katherine Marie born 6 May 1908.[155]

Timothy and Jane began their marriage in a small two story house on Church Street owned by Timothy's parents.[156] John Clark resided with them. The house, which is still standing is located on a tiny lot close to the street. During the period Timothy and Jane occupied the house, railroad tracks ran in the rear of the property.

The elder McCarthys owned six properties on Church Street. The house in which Jennie and Timothy resided passed to Timothy's sister Anna upon the death of their mother.[157] However, Timothy inherited the bulk of the remaining properties; three houses and a barn.[158] The lot plan shows the properties are located across the street from an "old cemetery."[159] I have visited Church Street several times to view the houses, but I have no recollection of a cemetery in the area. St. John the Baptist Church was located on the corner of Church and King Street until that later part of the century when the church was razed. The cemetery may have been moved at that time.

Calm presided over the family for an extended period, until the passing of William Conners in Buckland, Massachusetts on 12 April 1901 at the age of forty-eight.[160]

Ten months later, John Clark succumbed on 10 February 1902 of heart disease and bronchitis.[161] He passed away in the McCarthy's Church Street residence. The death was reported by the *Daily Hampshire Gazette* on the same day: "John Clark, aged 61, died this morning at the home of his daughter, Mrs. Timothy McCarthy of Church Street, of a complication of diseases. Mr. Clark was born in Ireland, but had lived in this city for a number of years being employed as a grinder in the Bay State Cutleries."[162]

John Clark's death certificate contained the names of both parents: Hugh Clark and Mary Carroll. This is the only documentation I have located that contains evidence of his mother's name.[163]

The information reported in the obituary contradicts the information supplied by John Clark in public records. His naturalization record states that he was born in Liverpool, England. This fact was reported by John himself to the court. However, to date, there is no known official record of his birth. It is not unusual to find errors such as this in obituaries.

John is interred at St. Mary's Cemetery on North Elm Street in Northampton with Hannah, William Conners and Jennie Doyle.

This was a difficult decade for both Jane and Timothy in terms of personal losses. Timothy's younger brother Patrick, died of pneumonia in Halifax, Nova Scotia on 7 March 1907.[164]

Three months later on 13 July 1907 his sister Catherine succumbed to tuberculosis.[165] Without question, the family was deeply touched by the losses. In November, Timothy, who had been dabbling in local politics, winning a seat as an alderman for the city, decided not to run for another term.[166] However, after lengthy hiatus, he returned to politics in 1917 as the treasurer of the democratic city committee in Northampton.

Ann Wallace Myers at an advanced age. Unfortunately, there are no
known photos of Hannah. Courtesy of Helen "Molly" Myers.

Patrick Myers memorial headstone at St. Mary's Cemetery in
Northampton. Patrick is interred at Old Calvary Cemetery
in Greenfield. Photograph by George Banas.

St. Mary's Cemetery, Northampton, Massachusetts.
Photograph by George Banas.

The timeworn Clark headstone at St. Mary's Cemetery in Northampton with inscriptions for John and Hannah. Photograph by George Banas.

Inscription for William Conners and Jennie Doyle on the Clark headstone. Who was Jennie Doyle? I have dedicated a chapter to her at the end of the book. Photograph by George Banas.

VI

Circumstances, Eventualities and Milestones

Jimmy was still excelling in track and field events in his mid-thirties. An article that appeared in the *Springfield Republican* in the 2 September 1902 edition, noted that he was the winner of the 100 yard dash (10 ¼ seconds), running hop, step, jump (40 ft. 8 inches) and three standing jumps (32 ft. 2 inches), at the labor unions' field day.[167] He placed second to Maurice Landry, a W.A. Bailey team member, in the running high jump.[168] Two days later the 14 September issue reported that he was the winner of three broad jump contests.[169]

The prize money he received as a local sports celebrity did not pay the bills and Jimmy continued to work at Billy Lee's cutlery shop. A job that provided a regular paycheck was vital. He had a growing family to support. Between 1895 and 1906, Mary Ann gave birth to six children; however, an unforeseen tragedy struck the family once again when an infant whom they named Joseph died shortly after birth due to strangulation by the umbilical cord.[170] Members of the Clark family I interviewed were unaware of this child. The location of his burial is unknown. This is a mystery, which I have written about at length. His story appears in a later chapter entitled: *The Mystery Infants: Joseph and Robert.*

Apart from the death of their infant son, there were other circumstances beyond the Clarks control, which undoubtedly caused stress and hardship during this period, as well. Between 1906 and 1907, there were intermittent strikes in the cutlery shops in Bay

State.[171] While there was a lack of financial stability in the Clark household throughout Jimmy and Mary Ann's marriage, the challenge of supporting a gaggle of five children on a reduced income with no certainty of when Jimmy could return to work must have been daunting. Jimmy may have been able to generate a small income through athletic competitions, but it would not have been nearly enough to support the household.

That being said, the W.A. Bailey team was still riding high well into the new century. A small item, which appeared in the 21 September 1905 edition of the *Springfield Republican*, was an indication of the team's status as local celebrities

"The W.A. Bailey and Haydenville running teams were leaving for the Greenfield Fair at 8:10 in the morning in a special electric car."[172]

There was so much fanfare surrounding Jimmy, it may have appeared to those outside of the family that Mary Ann was the little woman standing silently on the sidelines; however comments from those who knew her tell a different story.

Mary Ann was the authority figure in the family. I do not think it could have been any other way in view of the fact that Jimmy held a full-time job at the cutlery and spent his spare time competing in athletic events. He was also a volunteer firefighter at the Bay State station. All of these activities would have left her alone to care for the children and manage the household. However, Jimmy's success as an athlete also meant additional income that was vital to the support of the family

Mary Ann's position as authority figure and general manager of the Clark household seemed to be the crux of many of the ensuing relationship issues with her children.

Cousin Jack Clark wrote that he thought his father (John G. Clark) held onto bitterness toward his mother, due to the fact that she encouraged her children to leave school and go to work. "Father, who was ambitious, always blamed his mother for forcing him to leave school. Certainly, he had a brief childhood. I'm not sure he ever forgave her as he tried to educate himself through reading in the public library."[173]

Historically, children of lower income families were often forced to leave school and find work to help support the household, and while Mary Ann bore all of the blame for denying her children an education, there were other forces at work in the "Village" that contributed to the circumstances pertaining to the children's early departure from school.

An examination of the 1910 census provides insight into the lives of the young boys of the "Village" who labored in the mills and factories and an interesting finding pertaining to their sisters.

A cursory survey of the Clark's neighborhood during the enumeration of 1910, which included Vernon Street, James Avenue, Federal Street and Main Street (Riverside Drive), where the Clark family resided, revealed that a majority of the teenage boys age fourteen and over were employed by a mill or a cutlery.[174] One male, aged thirteen was employed as a cutlery inspector.[175] Indeed, this enumeration revealed that Leo, age 14, worked as a laborer at a silk mill.[176] His entry indicated that he had not attended school since September 1, 1909.[177]

Apparently, the trend of sending children to work in local manufactories did not extend to females, who for the most part remained in school. Interestingly, most teenage females enumerated in the neighborhood were still attending school at age seventeen. I found this dichotomy of the sexes surprising and worthy of future study.

Since this practice appeared to be widespread and "normal" in the culture of the cutlery village, James and Mary had no reason to ponder ethics or suffer guilt for sending their sons to work instead of school. Still, looking at the cutlery village culture from the distance of one hundred years, it would appear that young males were denied a basic education in order to subsidize the household; a responsibility based solely on their gender.

It is unknown how long Mae and Nell remained in school. However, it clear that the lack of an education had a devastating effect upon John and Leo, which became more evident over time.

Apart from the cultural influences of the cutlery village, religion also played a major role in the lives of the Clark children. Both Jimmy and Mary were devout Catholics and active members of the local church. The church played a central role in the lives of the majority of Irish Catholics due to the imposition of the penal laws by the British government, which denied generations of Catholics the right to practice their religion. The Penal Laws also denied Catholics the right to vote and restricted their ability to attain wealth, among other things. While the laws were gradually repealed over time, they were not entirely repealed until 1920.[178] Having been denied the right to practice their religion, the Irish embraced their faith with fervor. Undoubtedly, the Clark children received many hours of religious instruction pertaining to the Roman Catholic Church's tenets of faith. Like generations before them, the principles of the church were ingrained in their psyche and ensconced in their daily walk. While I do not have knowledge of the religious practices of all of the Clark children over their lifetimes, taking into consideration all of the evidence pertaining to this family, it is clear that Mae, John and Leo remained faithful to the Roman Catholic Church. I do not know if Helen (Nellie) and William continued to practice their faith.

History has been kinder to Jimmy than to Mary Ann. However, no one is perfect. I have heard rumors from an assortment of relatives over the course of time that Jimmy sometimes drank heavily. Apparently, this was an intermittent problem throughout his life. My grandmother Mae told me that her father once came home drunk from a night out and threw a boot at her. Her brief account of that event left her in tears. She never disclosed the details of what transpired after the boot was tossed at her, but I am certain there was more to the story. Still, I can say without hesitation that Mae loved her father. She always spoke of him in a respectful manner.

Her comments centered on his talent as an athlete and his popularity in Northampton. Apparently, she believed his spirit was close to her. She was known to say that when a death was about to occur in the family, he would come to her in a dream.

Mae's boot story notwithstanding, nearly every tale told about Jimmy Clark portrays him as a doting father and grandfather. Cousin Jack wrote that in early childhood his father (John G. Clark) was admitted to Cooley Dickinson Hospital to undergo surgery for removal of his tonsils; however following the procedure, his bleeding could not be controlled and he was transferred to another area of the hospital known as the "scarlet room." Jimmy was summoned and advised that if he wanted to see John alive, he should go to the hospital immediately. According to the account, Jimmy ran a half mile to the hospital and upon arrival, he was so shaken, he had to hold onto the fence for support."[179]

John G. was not the only Clark child to suffer a potentially deadly childhood illness. Mae told me she suffered a bout with scarlett fever, a much feared childhood disease caused by the streptococcus virus.[180] A common treatment for the disease required that the patient's hair be cut and unfortunately little Mae's long black curls had to be sheared off. Apparently, all items that belonged to the patient, including the sheared locks, were burned in the belief that it would stop the disease from spreading.[181] I was left with the impression that having her hair cut was more traumatic than the disease. She did not tell me how her parents reacted to her illness.

The only story Mae shared with me regarding everyday life in the James Clark household was her description of her mother heating water on the stove on Friday night and pouring it into a big brass basin in the middle of the kitchen floor for Jimmy to bath in. She complained that her father was: "...so dirty!"[182]

Both Mary Ann and Jimmy maintained relationships with their extended family throughout this period. However, over the years, the Cashman family scattered. Maud and Dan both had hotel businesses in different states and Roger was somewhere in the West. Mary Ann's heart and concerns were always with her brother Roger. He returned to Northampton occasionally and wrote sporadically. She missed him tremendously. Even in her old age, she often spoke of him. Her sister Julia was the only sibling that lived nearby. Her parents lived with Julia and her husband John Foran on Park Street in Florence.

Unfortunately, it was a death in the family that brought the Cashman family together. Mary Ann's father, Cornelius Cashman passed on 21 April 1915 of influenza and endocarditis.[183] When the family gathered for the funeral, Roger was the only sibling who did not attend. Cornelius' obituary stated that he was residing in the West.[184] Roger lived in both California and Nevada during this period. His absence from the funeral may have been due to the fact that the family did not know his address.

At the time of Cornelius' death, Leo and Mae were in their late teens. John and William were growing up quickly, as well. When I speak of this generation of Clark's I am always hesitant. The challenges Jimmy and Mary's children faced as they traveled through adulthood were akin to the experiences of their immigrant grandparents. The future that loomed before them included a devastating economic disaster and two wars. And there were other issues that dogged the Clark children. The problems were personal and close to their hearts. How this generation coped with their insecurities and anxieties was at times both sad and amusing.

My grandmother Mae was the eldest daughter and the first to marry. She never told me how she and Grandpa Wilbur Cleary met, so it came as a bit of shock when I discovered he was boarding in a rented house with the Clarks on Riverside Drive in 1915.[185]

Wilbur always told his grandchildren that he was an orphan. He also claimed he had an uncle who was judge and that he spent his summers on his estate in Holyoke, Massachusetts. One afternoon while perusing old photos with Mae, I came upon a picture of a large magnificent house that was labeled: "Judge Cleary's Summer Estate." When I asked if the house in the photo was the same house Wilbur spent his summers, Mae laughed and told me, he was joking.

The photo of what I perceived to be a large magnificent house was among some old pictures my mother, Anne (Cleary) Goodhind passed on to me a number of years ago. Not long ago, I took out the photo to examine it and upon closer inspection I realized that it was a photo of the Springfield Armory. Yes, Wilbur was a joker! His claim that he was an orphan was another embellishment.

Wilbur's birth record states that he was born on 27 October 1893 to Andrew Cleary and Margaret Cashion in Bennington, New Hampshire.[186] Research revealed that both parents were alive, well into his adulthood.[187]

Perhaps Wilbur felt like an orphan. He was separated from his family for an extensive period of time, early in his life. His mother, who was often sick, suffered from epilepsy.[188] At a young age, Wilbur traveled to Norfolk, Virginia with his Aunt Margaret (Cleary) and her husband August Lachman.[189] He lived in Norfolk with the Lachmans, along with his uncle "Jack" Cleary, for approximately ten years.[190]

Wilbur had a younger sister named Ave Maria, who was known by the locals in Bennington as "Ave". Ave, like her mother, suffered from epilepsy. Mae's eldest daughter Peg, spent several summers at the Cleary household in Bennington. She said Ave was born with a "wry neck" and a problem with one of her arms, which appeared to be deformed.[191] From time to time, she was transported to the state hospital in Concord for treatment.[192]

It is unknown why Wilbur relocated to Bay State Village. However, the Cashmans were connected to Bennington, New Hampshire through Mary Ann's older sister Ellen and her husband Edward Holloran, who lived there for a short time.[193] The neighboring Dobler family also residents of the "Village." were transplants from Bennington, as well.[194] It is likely Grandpa Wilbur came to Northampton vis à vis his relationship with one or both families.

Wilbur was nicknamed "Cappy" because of his affinity for hats. He was employed by William and Rogers LTD in Florence.

Mae never talked about their courtship, but she did share that she came down with the flu just a week before she and Wilbur were to be married. She told me she was very sick and that she felt so cold she wanted "to crawl into the oven." She lost bit of weight due to the illness, but she managed to recover in time to walk down the aisle of Blessed Sacrament Church on 17 April 1917.[195] The Daily Hampshire Gazette reported the wedding:

> The Party entered the church to the strains of the Mendelassohn [sic] wedding march and during the ceremony Miss Barbara Carter sang "O Promise Me," and "O Salutaris." The couple were attended by Miss Helen Clark, a sister of the bride and Walter Cleary of Milford, N.H., a cousin of the groom. The ushers were Leo Clark, a brother of the bride and Walter Dobler. The bride was charming in a Copenhagen blue suit with black hat and corsage bouquet of bridal roses and gardenias. Her attendant wore a darker blue suit with black hat and pink sweet peas. A wedding breakfast was served at the home of the bride's parents, after which Mr. and Mrs. Cleary left on a wedding trip to Boston and New Hampshire.[196]

Mae and Wilbur moved several times in the early years of their marriage. However, after the birth of their first child, they resided with Jimmy and Mary Ann.

Wilbur secured a job at the Armory in Springfield, Massachusetts, where he worked the night shift for short time. During that period he was also employed by the William and Rogers Company and Clement Manufacturing. Eventually, Wilbur and Mae settled on Middle Street in Florence in a duplex or double house, as they were called in that era. Wilbur was employed by the International

Silver Company on the corner of Maple and Middle Streets until his retirement.

The Middle Street address was home to the family for many years. Wilbur grew vegetables and cultivated beautiful flowers during the warm months. Mae cooked and cared for the children and later her mother and their grandchildren. Both Mae and Wilbur were avid readers. Wilbur also enjoyed writing songs and poetry. He penned a poem about a fallen soldier, which was published in *Readers Digest*. While I saw a copy of the poem years ago, I do not remember the title. To date, I have not located a copy of the work.

In 1960, they moved from the double house on Middle Street, where they had lived and raised their children for the greater part of the marriage, and relocated to Monson. Shortly thereafter they moved to Palmer to care for the children of their daughter Helene (Cleary) Polom, who passed away in the early 1960s.[197]

Wilbur and Mae had five children: Margaret (Peg), Roger, Helene, Anne Marie (Annie) and Edward (Eddie).[198]

Wilbur died at home on 27 October 1964.[199] It was his 71st birthday. He suffered a stroke while napping after lunch, after working in the yard. Mae passed on 13 July 1993 in Hampden, Massachusetts.[200] She had been residing in a nursing home for several years. She died of natural causes.

Left to right: Wilbur Cleary and Walter Dobler.
Standing: Walter Cleary.

Wilbur and Mae on their wedding day.

Mae with baby Anne (1932).

Wilbur claimed this was Judge Cleary's estate. Upon closer inspection, it became apparent this photo is an image of the Springfield Armory.

VII

World War I

Mae's marriage to Wilbur Cleary in April 1917 and the subsequent birth of their first child the following February may have been the only high note in the lives of the Clarks for many years to come.[201] A month after their wedding, the Selective Act[202] was enacted due to a conflict ignited by the assassination of Archduke Franz Ferdinand and his wife in Sarejevo.[203] Subsequently, war was declared on Serbia by Austria and Hungary. Eventually the conflict grew into World War I. The United States held a neutral position until 6 April 1917, when it declared war on Germany.[204]

Leo reported to the local Draft Board for registration on 5 June 1917, two weeks prior to his 22nd birthday.[205] Registrants for the draft were required to fill out a card, which posed questions pertaining to the potential draftee's address, vital statistics, employment and physical features. Leo's entries on the registration card noted that he was employed by William A. Rogers LTD, a silver manufacturing company that produced flatware and other items.[206]

His address was entered as Riverside Drive.[207] The physical description noted he was of medium height and slender with black hair and gray eyes.[208]

Registering for the draft was not a guarantee that Leo would be called to service, but undoubtedly Mary Ann and Jimmy were anxious about what lay ahead for their eldest son. However, if the Clarks were anxious, the Becketts and the McCarthys were jittery as well. Both Raymond and Edward Beckett were required to register for the draft, though in separate registrations.[209] Raymond, the youngest of the pair, was not eligible to register, until the third registration period in September 1918.[210] Edward registered in June 1917, shortly after his marriage to Elizabeth "Besse" McElroy.[211] Edward's physical description on the registration card was nearly identical to Leo's. It noted that he too, had black hair and gray eyes.[212] Unfortunately, Raymond's card was illegible, due to a poor quality image. Both Beckett brothers were employed by the railroad when they filed for the draft.[213] There is no record of either brother serving in the military.

John P. McCarthy, Jane and Timothy's eldest son was also required to register for the draft. His draft card noted that he resided at his parent's address on 13 Church Street in Northampton.[214] The entry for his occupation states that he was employed as a printer by H.S. Gere and Sons, owners of the *Daily Hampshire Gazette*, on Gothic Street in Northampton.[215] John's physical description on his draft card was similar to that of his cousins. However, while it is stated that he had black hair, his eye color was entered as "brown."[216]

According to the records of the Adjutant Generals Office, John was a member of the Students' Army Training Corp (SATC) at Holy Cross College in Worcester.[217]

During this period, the federal government utilized college campuses as training camps to prepare students for military service. John was inducted into the army on 18 October 1918.[218] He received an honorable discharge approximately two months later on 14 December 1918.[219] His record does not contain an explanation for his discharge.[220]

Leo was called to duty the following year.[221] On Monday, 28 May 1918, he was inducted into the Army and transported to Camp Upton (Long Island) for basic training.[222]

Leo left school at an early age, in order to work and help support the family. In that respect, Leo entered adulthood long before he lived out his childhood. However, Leo was not a man of the world when he boarded the train in Springfield for Camp Upton in preparation for basic training. It is likely he had only traveled the distance from Bay State to Providence to visit his cousins. Moreover, Bay State was an insular place to grow up, a small world where everyone knew his or her neighbor. Undoubtedly, both he and his family suffered a great deal of anxiety knowing he would be in dangerous territory and that he might not return to them.

Upon his completion of basic training, he was transferred to Camp Greenleaf, Georgia where he trained for the medical corp. Soon after he was transferred to Italy for the duration of his enlistment. Certainly, Leo was exposed to some horrendous sights while treating the injured soldiers in the combat zone. Family members would later say the war changed his personality.

While the Vittorio Vineto offensive (24 October 1918-November 1918) [223] marked the end of the war, Leo spent nearly five additional months based in Italy. [224]

His tour of duty concluded with an honorable discharge from the army at Fort Devens on 30 April 1919. [225]

Mae's husband Wilbur was not drafted, but he longed to join the military and at one point he attempted to enlist. I am sure this was very upsetting to Mae since they were just beginning a family when the war erupted. Wilbur was rejected for military service because of his height. He was just five feet, two inches tall. [226]

Leo Clark in full regalia c. 1917.

VIII

And It All Fell Down...

When Leo returned from the service he found the village as he left it. However, there were changes in the Clark household. Mae and Wilbur had moved to their own residence and Nell, his free-spirited little sister, was involved in a serious relationship with Walter Dobler.

Nell and Walter probably knew each other since childhood. Walter was born in Bennington, New Hampshire on 22 March 1898 to Ferdinand Dobler and his wife, Josephine Mier, immigrants from Switzerland.[227] The family relocated to Northampton circa 1902, as his father Ferdinand is listed in city directories at various addresses from that year onward.[228] Walter's father was also a cutlery worker, first at Clement Manufacturing and then at the Northampton Cutlery, which was located in Bay State on the Mill River.

Interestingly, the Doblers and Wilbur's family were found living in the same neighborhood in Bennington in the 1900 census.[229] However, since Wilbur spent much of his childhood in Norfolk, Virginia with relatives, they may not have become acquainted with one another until Wilbur moved to Bay State.

Walter was serving in the Navy at the same time Leo was serving in Army. It was during his enlistment that Walter's friendship with Nell blossomed into a serious relationship. It is hard to imagine Nell, at that stage of her life, settling down.

When I think of Nell, I remember her as an elderly woman, in the nineteen-sixties when she made infrequent, but lengthy visits to Mae in Palmer, Massachusetts. I have never met anyone who could talk as much and as fast as Aunt Nell. I know of no one else in the family who possessed a similar temperament or personality. Walter, on the other hand, was reserved. He and Wilbur would sit in the living room together and barely say a word to one another.

Nell and Walter were married on January 31, 1920 in Northampton.[230] Unfortunately, an announcement for the wedding was not available.

Prior to their marriage Nell was employed as a housemaid at one of the colleges, probably Smith College.[231] Walter, like many of the local men, who were looking for a bigger pay check,, took a job at the Armory in Springfield after his discharge from the Navy.[232] He boarded in Springfield at the residence of Annie E. Bickford.[233] It is likely he returned to his family on the weekends.

It appeared that immediately after the marriage Walter was still boarding in Springfield, while Nell remained in the Clark residence;[234] however, they were found living as a couple on Niagra Street in Springfield in the years 1924-1927.[235] Eventually, they relocated to Hartford, where Walter was employed by Colt Manufacturing.[236] They remained in the Hartford area for the balance of their lives.[237] One child whom they named Phylis was born to Walter and Nell.[238] Nell died on 24 September 1979 in Wethersfield, Connecticut.[239] Walter passed on 5 November 1981 in Newington, Connecticut.[240]

It appears that early 1920-1922 was a happy period in the Clark family. Leo had completed his tour of duty. Nell and Walter married and Mae gave birth to a baby boy on 30 January 1920, just one day before the Doblers nuptials.[241] They named the baby Roger, after Mary Ann's brother, Roger Cashman. Roger was the Clarks first grandson.

The following year, Mary Ann and Jimmy were able to purchase the small cottage style house they had been renting from Clement

Manufacturing.[242] Interestingly, three days after the recording, Jimmy transferred the property to Mary Ann.[243] The Riverside Drive property was the first and only house they owned.

The news was good until 1922. However, when Mae gave birth to her third child, something went awry. I do not know the details of what occurred, but I do know that Mae was confined to the hospital for months due to a bone infection in her leg, which resulted in a lack of mobility in her right knee.[244] She walked with a limp for the rest of her life. Mae told me that she was in pain almost constantly. It was common to find her messaging her knee with a distressed expression. I have been told the disability changed her personality.

Peg, known as "Peggy Baum" to the family and Roger were sent to live with Mary Ann and Jimmy for the duration of Mae's illness.[245] However, I have no knowledge of the whereabouts of the new baby, a girl named Helene. Since Peg never mentioned the baby living with Mary Ann and Jimmy, I always assumed the infant remained in the hospital with Mae.

While Mae was in desperate straits with her heath issues, Peg and Roger were well taken care of by their grandparents. From Peg's description of life on Riverside Drive, it was a great adventure. She said the Clarks had a backyard farm where Mary cultivated a garden and Jimmy raised chickens.[246]

She told me Jimmy would dress her up in an old pair of oversized pants with a rope tied around the waist and together they would walk to Paradise Pond on the Smith College campus;[247] a panacea for her childhood asthma. Vigorous exercise can sometimes induce an asthma attack. Fortunately, this was not the case with Peg. She enjoyed the walks and never mentioned any ill effects from the exercise.

Mary Ann was not always in accord with Jimmy's idea of suitable entertainment for Peg and Roger. On occasion, much to the annoyance of Mary Ann, he would take Peg and Roger into the bedroom and teach them to box.[248] While Mary Ann was opposed to Jimmy's attempt to entertain the children by engaging them in a potentially dangerous sport, learning to box was a happy memory that Peg recited to me many times. She adored her grandfather and from her accounts of their relationship, he adored her. She described him as a "magnificent man with black hair and very light skin." [249] She spoke with great love and respect for both of her grandparents.

While Mary Ann and Jimmy enjoyed their grandchildren, they were not without their personal issues. Jimmy still enjoyed consuming a few drinks with his friends at the local bars. Peg said: "He would go out on weekend nights with his co-worker Ed Hannifin, who lived down the street. They would have a few drinks and then they would dance. They would dance in the bar and dance all the way home. Grandma made no bones about her dislike for this kind of activity."[250]

While Jimmy had occasional issues with alcohol, Mary Ann was not a model of perfection. She had a penchant for shoes. Even when she had little money to spare, she would head to the center to purchase shoes on payday.[251] I do not know if her obsession with footwear became problematic. Photos of her that span several decades show her wearing shoes of the same style that were typically worn by older women of the time.

Mae was still struggling to recover from the infection, when Thomas Conners, Jimmy's half brother, was admitted to Cooley Dickinson Hospital. He died on 16 November 1922 of cancer.[252] He left his wife, Nora (McCarthy). I do not know the status of Jimmy's relationship with Thomas. However, Thomas named his first and only son "James."[253]

I have included the biographies of Thomas and his brother William in a later chapter.

By early 1920, Jimmy and Mary Ann and their three sons were occupying the house on Riverside Drive. At least three of the four males living in the household were gainfully employed. It is unclear if William was working.

It was during this period that Leo met and eventually married Margaret Casey. However, the wedding was almost called off because of a family issue. Leo had been training to be a jeweler and was saving money to start a business in Northampton when his mother asked him for a loan to pay back taxes on the family home. The loan was never repaid. This caused a great deal of strife between the couple and Margaret nearly called off the wedding. [254]

Margaret did not have a carefree childhood. She weathered some difficult circumstances and major losses early in life. Her father Michael, who was employed by his aunt (Ellen Whalen), on her farm in Hadley, Massachusetts lost his job due to the foreclosure of the property. The family's situation was further exacerbated when her mother died on 22 March 1911.[255] Margaret was just ten years old at the time. Four months after her mother's death, Ellen Whalen died.[256] Even more painful, was the departure of her father from her life. At some point, her father Michael had a disagreement with his brother John and his wife Lizzie regarding the care of the Casey children. It came to pass that Margaret and her siblings were then moved to John and Lizzie's house on Walnut Street in Northampton, where the couple cared for them into adulthood. Her father moved to Connecticut and effectively abandoned his children. They never heard from him again. They did not know where he was or what became of him until they were notified of his death in 1949.[257]

The Casey children's disappointments did not end when their father left them. When Ellen Whalen died she left a small legacy to each of the children that was embezzled by the manager of the account. It is unclear if the thief was prosecuted. However, I have been told that the money from the legacies was never recovered.[258]

Whatever traumas occurred in her past, Margaret must have had sufficient confidence in her fiancé, to transcend the anguish of her childhood and look to the future. Leo and Margaret were married on 3 September 1923 in Northampton, Massachusetts.[259] The couple went to housekeeping at the Walnut Street property with Margaret's aunt, Lizzie Casey.

Eventually, Margaret purchased the Walnut Street property after the death of Lizzie Casey. However, the sale was not without issues. Lizzie died intestate and in debt to Margaret and her siblings.[260]

Margaret's only option, in order to remain in the house, was to purchase the property from the estate at a public auction.[261] While she was able to recover some of the money she had loaned her aunt from the estate, she paid a handsome sum for the property.[262]

Leo and Margaret resided in the house on Walnut Street for the duration of their marriage. They had three daughters: Mary, Patricia and Cathleen.[263] Leo is best remembered by his family for his green thumb. He cultivated beautiful gardens on the Walnut Street property and enjoyed sharing the flowers he harvested with his family. Leo died on 20 May 1968.[264] Margaret died on 28 June 2001.[265]

It would seem there was little breathing space between births, deaths and marriages during the nineteen-twenties. Less than a year after Leo and Margaret's marriage, Mary Ann's mother passed (Bridget Cashman) on 21 November 1924.[266] She was eight-five years old at the time of her death.[267] It is unclear if the Clark children were close to their grandmother. Bridget lived with Mary Ann's sister Julia, and her husband John Foran on Park Street in Florence for many years.

It is likely that all of the Cashman children gathered for the funeral. The family continued to communicate with one another over the years. However, Roger's correspondence with the family was sporadic and for the most part the Cashman family had no idea where he was or if he was alive. I have been told by several family members that Mary Ann was deeply affected by his absence from her life. The mystery of what happened to her brother would follow her to the end of her life.

Just four months after Bridget Cashman passed, Mary Ann's older sister Ellen died in New Britain at the age of fifty-eight.[268] She left behind a husband and a large family. I have been told,

Ellen was a beloved sister. Her death was a huge loss for the family.

Beyond the many deaths that occurred in this period, life was changing for all of the Clarks. The children were growing up quickly. By 1925, Edward,[269] Florence[270] and Annie Beckett had married.[271] Mary,[272] age 18, and Ruth, age 14, were still at home.[273] Raymond, age 24, was also at home.[274]

Jane's oldest child, John had married sometime in 1924.[275] Anna[276] and Timothy[277] were of age and her youngest, child Catherine was seventeen years old.[278]

Jimmy's sons, John[279] and William[280] were still living at home. However, both were of age. Leo, Mae and Nell were married and living elsewhere.

All was well for the Clarks and the McCarthys; however in Providence, another tragedy was brewing.

Mamie Beckett suffered a stroke on 3 December 1925. She died at home at 8:00 AM on 9 December.[281] She was fifty-seven years old.

I have been told that twins have a stronger emotional bond than most siblings. I cannot imagine Jimmy's anguish upon hearing of Mamie's passing. Her death may well have been a factor in his own demise.

Subsequent to Mamie's death, there is little to be gleaned from public records pertaining to this family. However, I have been told that Raymond, known as "Ray" owned a nightclub and had ties to the entertainment industry.[282] He eventually married Bertha C. Anderson on 21 January 1932 in Manhattan, New York.[283] Edward and his wife, Besse, owned a house in Onset, Massachusetts, which was the site of family gatherings.[284]

I have very little additional information pertaining to this family. However, it can be said that the Beckett family stayed in contact with their Massachusetts kin. Evidence of this can be found in old photos scattered throughout the family that span decades and obituaries which note that Raymond and Edward served as pall bearers at family funeral services.

The six surviving Beckett children lived to maturity:

Annie (Beckett) Ennis died in September 1980 in Providence Rhode Island.[285] Raymond died in March 1986 in Providence, Rhode Island.[286] Florence (Beckett) Selwyn died in September 1974 in Providence, Rhode Island.[287] Mary Gertrude died in 1973 in Hopkinton, Rhode Island.[288]

Ruth (Beckett) Morrissey passed in 1993 in Warwick, Rhode Island.[289] Edward J. (Jr.) died c. 1964.[290]

Edward J. Beckett Sr. never remarried. He died on 28 April 1946 in Providence, Rhode Island.[291]

Unfortunately, this is where my knowledge of this family ends.

Certainly, Mamie's death was a huge emotional blow to the Clarks. However, it was not the end of a long string of death and tragedies which beset the family during this decade.

Mary Ann's sister, Maud (Cashman) Miller, fell while stepping off a trolley in Northampton on a snowy winter day. According to Peg Leitl, "her spinal cord was severed and she never walked again."[292]

Maud was living in Rochester, New York at the time of the accident. She had no children or spouse. Her first husband, James Wheeler, a hotel owner in Winchester, Connecticut, died in 1907.[293] Her second husband, John J. Miller, passed on 17 April 1922 in Rochester, New York.[294] John was a banker and the owner of both the Kenmore Hotel and a bar in Rochester.[295] I have been told the couple also owned an establishment on Block Island.[296] Obviously, Maud was accustomed to a high lifestyle.

However, after a limited recovery, she sold the hotel in Rochester and moved to Jimmy and Mary Ann's modest home on Riverside Drive, where she remained until the late 1920s.

Peg told me that Maud was dedicated to making a full recovery. To that end, she traveled to St. Anne De Beaupre, a Canadian church renowned for healings and attended social events in Northampton. It would appear she kept a busy schedule.[297]

Maud possessed a theatrical quality and apparently, she dressed to impress. Peg said that upon meeting her, she could not take her eyes off her red wig and mink coat. She also spoke of Maud's elaborately decorated bedroom that was furnished with gilt furniture.[298] However, there was also a grittier side to Maud. Leo, who worked for her briefly, told his family that Maud smuggled liquor from Canada into the United States under her skirts, while posing in a wheel chair.[299] From all that I have been told about Maud, she was not unlike Mary Ann and Julia, who had very different sides to their personalities that were apparent only to those, who knew them well.

The daily grind must have been more interesting with Maud in residence. Beyond that, she was an affluent woman. Certainly some of the financial limitations of the Clarks' were lifted by her contributions to the household.

It was during this period that John met Ruth Miller, a pretty blonde of German extraction from Easthampton.[300] Ruth was born on 8 January 1902 to Minnie Hupher and Frances (Frank) Miller.[301] The Millers were an industrious family. Minnie worked in a suspender mill, prior to the marriage and Frank worked alongside his father in a tailoring shop.[302] Frank later owned his own shop in Easthampton.[303] Interestingly, the Miller and Hupher lived next door to each other.[304]

Ruth's family was close knit and apparently, they had a high regard for education. Ruth completed high school and went on to attend Northampton Commercial College.[305]

It is apparent that there were differences in John's and Ruth's backgrounds and ethnicities. Those differences were never issues for the Clarks. However, the difference in their religious associations was a cause for concern. The Millers were Protestants and the Clarks were devout Roman Catholics. It has been said that there was tension within the Clark family over the marriage.[306] It is likely the Clarks' angst was based on Roman Catholic doctrine regarding interfaith marriages. Canon law requires that "mixed" couples receive permission from the bishop in order to marry. During the period Ruth and John married, the laws were more stringent and such unions were uncommon. The laws are no longer as strict, as they once were, but even today, permission is required for a Catholic to marry a non-Catholic.[307] The details of what occurred between John, the Clark family and the Church when he announced his plans to marry Ruth is lost in the ethers. However, it is likely they were married in a civil ceremony in Connecticut because of the church's restrictions on interfaith marriages.

John and Ruth tied the knot on 3 January 1927 in Somerville, Connecticut.[308] The wedding announcement did not include details of the service.[309]

Once married, Ruth attended the Catholic Church. According to her daughter-in-law Andrienne (Goggin) Clark: "Ruth gave up her religion for her husband's sake. To my knowledge, she never attended religious services at the Congregational Church after she was married."[310]

I met Ruth just a few times over the years. My impression of her was that of a calm, sensible woman. I never heard anyone in the family speak of her in a disparaging manner.

Over her long marriage to John, Ruth wore many hats, both professionally and personally. She was employed by the Northampton Institute for Savings and during World War II, both she and John worked at the Springfield Armory.[311] Later she worked at United Elastic in Easthampton.[312] Ruth also helped John run the dairy farm they bought in 1940 and during his tenure in the House of Representatives, she served as his local secretary.[313]

Although, I did not know John very well, it has become clear through my research of this family that he was not cut from the same cloth as his siblings. I do not know what characteristic or personality trait he possessed that propelled him forward throughout his life, despite a multitude of setbacks. However, even though he did not finish school due to his family's circumstances, he was able to enter law school in the mid-nineteen twenties. By the time he met Ruth, he was employed as an insurance agent. [314] John persevered and in the 1960s with Ruth by his side, he was elected to the Massachusetts House of Representatives.[315]

To my knowledge, the influences that inspired John to seek a career in politics have never been discussed. A fact worthy of thought is that the Clarks lived approximately one mile from Calvin Coolidges' residence on Massasoit Street. Mae told me she rode the same trolley with him to work. Julia (Cashman) Foran worked in a dress shop that Mrs. Coolidge frequented. She was well acquainted with the First Lady.[316]

I have never heard the Coolidge name mentioned in connection with John, who was a lifelong Democrat, but certainly, he knew that the President of the United States lived nearby. To date, there is no evidence to link the family's familiarity with the Coolidges' to John's interest in politics. However, it seems likely that a local attorney's rise to prominence through a career in politics would have made John aware that serving in public office was a viable option, even for an unknown young man from Bay State Village.

John and Ruth lived in Easthampton at the Miller home on Briggs Street for several years after their marriage.[317] Subsequently, they moved several times before purchasing a farm in Easthampton, where they remained for the balance of their lives.[318]

John and Ruth had one child, whom they named John Paul, born 29 April 1930.[319] However, within the family he was known as Jack. I have referred to him in this narrative as Cousin Jack.

While there was little support for John and Ruth's marriage, upon Cousin Jack's birth, there appeared to be a change in at least some family members attitudes.

A letter pertaining to his birth was recently discovered by his widow Andrienne Clark, while organizing items for the John G. Clark Collection at the W.E.B. Dubois Library at the University of Massachusetts. A cache of congratulatory cards and a letter from Maud (Cashman) Miller to John and Ruth were found in an antique purse which belonged to Ruth. Within the text of the letter Maud referred to John P. as "Jack", which was his nickname as well. Maud wrote:

May 14, 1930

Congratulations Jack, Ruth and the boy. My how proud we are. I can see Jack with his hat on the back of his head and hands in pckets [sic.]. Tomie [sic.] stuck out strutting along saying see what we got. Just look at this for a boy. Well I am awful glad it is a boy and Ruth is fine. I suppose your home by this time. Ruth [sic.] We were all glad to have the good tidings and hope to see you all soon...It must be hard on Jack to have to get up so early in the mornings but he must work hard now for the boy. Say Ruth I don't think you could do better in a name then call him Jack. This is my favorite name for a man. Well everyone is well here and we all wish you the best of luck...[320]

This letter seems to indicate that at least some of the Clark relations had come to accept the marriage.

When John married Ruth in 1927, the only Clark child remaining in the family home on Riverside Drive was William. By then, he had reached the age of majority and was gainfully employed.[321] This was fortunate. What lay ahead would devastate the family both spiritually and financially.

On 23 June 1927, Jimmy Clark celebrated his fifty-ninth birthday.[322] It would be his last.

Two bazaar incidents preceded his death. I first learned of these events through my Grandmother Mae, who shared the eerie occurrences with me and a group of cousins gathered around the kitchen table in Palmer one evening after dinner many years ago. According to Mae, the first incident occurred a few days before his death in August. She stated that after returning home from work in the afternoon, Jimmy reported that a pack of wild dogs followed him home. The second incident occurred one morning, as he stepped out of the house on Riverside Drive and reportedly, saw a vision of the Virgin Mary. According to Mae, Jimmy told her the Blessed Mother was dressed in a blue robe and was very beautiful. She cried, as she related this narrative to us.[323]

I have been told by cousins in Ireland that many of the Irish report visions of the Virgin Mary just prior to death. The cousins had no explanation for this phenomenon.

I have no knowledge of Jimmy's symptoms or if he had been feeling ill. He was admitted to Cooley Dickinson Hospital on 20 August 1927.[324] He passed two days later due to double lobar pneumonia.[325]

When I read this diagnosis, I was not surprised. Jimmy had spent his most of his life working in a cutlery, inhaling air that was infused with metal particles. Many men, women and children died prematurely as a result of the unhealthy working conditions that were prevalent in manufacturing facilities during that period.

Jimmy's obituary ran in the Daily Hampshire Gazette on 23 August 1927. It noted that: "As a youth he was one of the best all around athletes of Hampshire County. He was captain of the W.A. Bailey Running Team, being particularly fast in the 100 yard dash and other sprints. He was also noted as a broad jumper."[326]

Jimmy was waked at the Clark home on Riverside Drive. Peg was still a child when Jimmy passed and she did not remember everything that occurred in the days after his death. Her most vibrant memory of the wake was stepping up to the casket to kiss her grandfather's face, at the insistence of Maud. This experience never left her.[327] No doubt, there was keening and caressing of the corpse. This was the way, the Irish mourned their loved ones in that era.

Jimmy was buried at St. Mary's Cemetery on Elm Street in Northampton on 25 August 1927.[328] Mae told me the funeral had a very large attendance.

A week later a tribute to Jimmy and his athletic talents appeared in the *Daily Hampshire Gazette*:

A friend and admirer of the late James Clark told us the following:

One of the greatest all-around athletes that ever wore a spiked shoe in Northampton passed on, with the death of James Clark of Bay State last week."

Two decades ago his fame as an athlete was known wherever field sports were held, not only in Northampton, but all over New England and other states where he went and competed.

Jimmy Clark, as he was called by his hundreds of friends, was, according to our informant, one of those real sportsmen who were absolutely on the level, his heart was always in his work and he was most loyal to his friends.

An idea of how good an athlete he was, may be had from his mark of 6 feet three inches, which he made in in the high jump in Philadelphia winning the event in a national meet in which were entered the best men in the country. He was equally good in the broad jump, hop, step and jump and the so-called hitch and kick.

His fame here in all these sports was great, but it was as a runner he captured the popular fancy, and it was as leader of the great bunch that composed the never-to-be-forgotten W.A Bailey's world champion hose running team, that he will be best remembered.

For five years this Northampton running team swept all before them at firemen's musters wherever they were held. And leading them always was the slender, but sinewy Jimmy Clark. And well might he lead for he was close to the ten seconds for the century every time he speeded over the 100 yard distance. According to Maurice Landry, who was a close second in all-around sports to Clark, and who was one of the sprinters on the Bailey team, Clark many times ran the century in ten seconds. The Bailey running team is holder of the world's record for 800 feet, which they made at Ware, Mass., and their mark has never been beaten.

It came to pass at field meets, at least in this section, that when Clark and Landry entered the other athletes withdrew to the sidelines and watched the pair from Bay State do their stuff.

The break-up of the Bailey running team was almost tragic when, at a cattle show, the team, with such runners as Fred Britten, of Fairview, one of the star sprinters of the day teamed with Clark and with the then holder of the mile record, Tom Carroll of Boston, as well as, Maurice Landry, Charlie ONeil, Tom Keneavy, Billy Chatel, Joe Tichy and other fine runners they swept down the course away ahead, in time, of any of the others, one of whom was Baileys' greatest rival, the John H. Ashe team of Chicopee Falls. But disaster that they had evaded came to them, for before over 15,000 people, the late J.A. Boudway, the fastest man who ever broke a coupling, failed for the first time in the teams history, to make the hitch and the that for five long years never met defeat, felt its sting for the first time. How much their heart was in their work was attested when many of them broke down and sobbed.

The team never raced again for various reasons, but to thousands memory will bring back the sinewy boy who so often led them to victory.[329]

Jimmy's death came without warning. The house on Riverside Drive must have felt cold and hollow without him. I do not know how family members reacted to his parting; however, I have vivid memories of trips to the cemetery with Mae and Wilbur when I was very young. By then, Jimmy had been dead for nearly three decades, however,

Mae was inconsolable each time she visited her parent's resting place. I do not think she ever came to terms with their deaths.

The Clarks were still feeling the sting of Jimmy's death, when little more than a month after his passing, Ruth's father, Frank Miller, died of bladder cancer on 30 September 1927.[330] Certainly, this was a heavy blow to Ruth and Jack, who were just starting their life together.

Maud remained in the Clark home after Jimmy's death. This was fortunate. Mary Ann was not on stable ground financially. Cousin Jack wrote: "Again, referring to family stories overheard when I was young, Grandmother went through Grandfather's insurance money, which was probably very tiny, quickly after his death..."[331] Indeed, the stories Cousin Jack overheard were correct. However, I do not believe the Clark siblings were ever aware of the devastating conclusion to Mary's financial issues.

While Mary Ann was sliding toward financial disaster, by coincidence or perhaps divine providence, a potentially deadly accident was averted when Thomas Wade, an unemployed widower from nearby Hinkley Street, walked by the Clark residence and intervened. The *Springfield Republican* reported:

> The other fire last night was started by a Christmas candle which ignited the curtains of a window in the house of Mrs. James Clark, 278 Riverside Drive, Bay State. Thomas Wade, who chanced to be passing the house saw the blazing curtains and rushing in tore them down. Nothing but the curtains caught fire and the firemen found that Mr. Wade had done their work by stamping out the fire that destroyed the curtains. The greater part of the damage was done by the scorching of the woodwork around the window and the wallpaper.[332]

The fire occurred on 26 December 1928.[333] It is unknown whether Mary Ann knew Thomas Wade.[334]

William continued to live with his mother and aunt. He worked and I assume he was contributing to the household.

I know very little about William's personality, but judging by photographs of him, he was a good looking man. It is not surprising that he caught the attention of a beautiful young woman named Nathalie Coffron. I have few details pertaining to Nathalie's life prior to her marriage to William; however, according to the Connecticut Department of Health records Nathalie was born in Maine on 16 October 1908.[335] According to her grandson, James Bills, her childhood was very sad. Apparently, she and her sister were placed in an orphanage in Maine after the death of their mother. Their father remarried and started another family. However, he never removed his daughters from the orphanage. Evidently, Nathalie did not hold onto any bitterness for her father. According to Jim: "... my grandmother took care of him for years before he died."[336]

I have seen photos of Nathalie turned out in an elegant coat with a fur collar and a matching bucket hat. She was positively striking. However, I have been told that the sentiments of the family were anything but positive, when it came to this union. Apparently, there was much blathering among relatives regarding Nathalie's dark hair and complexion. I do not know how the couple reacted to the family's apparent bias.

The Clark sibling's attempt to thwart William and Nathalie's relationship with gossip and assumptions about her ethnicity was an indication that the family had begun to unravel. The Clark children now found excuses to find fault with one another at every turn. Their bitterness was manifested through mindless spats, gossip and persistent feuds.

However, the family's opposition to their relationship did not dampen their enthusiasm for each other. They were married on 13 July 1929, in Northampton and began a family almost immediately. [337] For the first few years of their marriage they lived with Mary Ann on Riverside Drive. [338] However, for most of their married life, they resided in or near Hartford, Connecticut.[339]

Eight children were born to Nathalie and William: James, William, Barbara, Thomas, Robert, Richard, Nathalie and Susan.[340] William died on 2 April 1961.[341] Nathalie died 25 May 1991.[342]

Both Nathalie and William passed in Hartford, Connecticut.[343]

Just months after William and Nathalie's wedding, the Great Depression struck. It struck with might, leaving in its wake, millions of people in financial ruin, years of high unemployment and untold suffering among the American working class.

All of Mary Ann and Jimmy's children faced adversity during this period. However, because of their youth and spiritual stamina, they were able to withstand the hard times. This was not the case for other family members, who suffered losses that were irreversible

It appears William did not lose his job during this period. A survey of city directories revealed that he was employed by the International Silver Company in Florence, until at least 1934.[344] Workers engaged in the manufacturing of metals and machinery earned considerably more than other factory workers. An average weekly wage was approximately $40.32[345] ($552.23 in 2013).[346] However, the pace of manufacturing declined to an extremely low level during the Depression. The city directory listings belie the fact that hourly rates and hours were cut during this period. It is likely that William's work hours were reduced and in turn, his paycheck was substantially less.

During this period Nathalie and William continued to reside on Riverside Drive with Mary Ann.[347]

Maud was not enumerated in the Clark household in the 1930 census taking.[348]

By then, she had relocated to Hartford, Connecticut, where she resided with Nell and Walter Dobler.[349]

With Maud in residence, the Doblers financial woes may have been less pressing than other family members'. Maud, who apparently made a very good living prior to the Depression, as a hotel and bar owner, still had some resources to draw upon, albeit limited resources.[350]

Leo, who toiled at William and Rogers LTD cutlery, walked to work each day.[351] When his shoes wore out, Margaret lined them with newspaper because they could not afford to have them repaired.[352] There is little doubt the family was managing on very little money at that time.

Undoubtedly, Maud's decision to move to Hartford, exacerbated Mary Ann's financial difficulties. No doubt her financial issues were at a critical level during this period.

Maud succumbed on 12 January 1932 at St. Francis Hospital in Hartford, Connecticut.[353] There was no cause of death cited on the death certificate; however, Mary Ann was named as the informant.[354] Apparently, Maud knew the end was near. Her will bears her signature and a date of 7 January 1932.[355] She left small legacies to her surviving sisters.[356] She also bequeathed small sums of money to some of her nieces and nephews. William and Leo were each bequeathed one hundred dollars.[357] Nell Dobler received two hundred dollars.[358] Mae's legacy was two hundred fifty dollars.[359] Her niece Margaret Foran was bequeathed a diamond ring.[360] Edward Holleran and his daughter Helen both received legacies, as well.[361] Times were tough financially for all members of the Clark family. Surely the money was a godsend to those who received the legacies.[362]

Things did not improve for Mary Ann after Maud's death. By 1934, she was having trouble making the mortgage payments on the house. She was not alone. Homeowners throughout the United States were struggling, due to the protracted economic downturn.

However, the future must have looked brighter to Mary Ann on 8 August 1934, when she secured a mortgage for fourteen hundred dollars from Home Owners' Loan Corporation.[363]

Jimmy and Mary Ann purchased the Riverside Drive property in 1920 for twelve hundred dollars.[364] Mary Ann received over $300 in excess of the loan payoff of the original mortgage, but it was too little, too late. Her financial difficulties deepened and the house was foreclosed on 20 December 1937.[365]

The house remained uninhabited until 1940, when it was sold by the Home Owners' Loan Corporation.[366]

While Mary Ann was dealing with the loss of her home, her sister-in-law Jane was dealing with the loss of her husband. Timothy McCarthy died on 9 May 1935 of hypertensive heart disease and nephritis. He was 64 years old.[367] He was waked at the family's residence on East Street in Northampton. The *Springfield Republican*'s 14 May 1935 edition, reported that four priests presided over the funeral celebration at St. Mary's Church with a "delegation from the Union of Plumbers and Steam and Gas Fitters" acting as "escorts."[368] Six members from the Knights of Columbus, honorary bearers along with six acting bearers also participated in the mass [sic].[369]

At the time of Timothy's death three of the four McCarthy children were married. John had married Marie Doyle in 1924.[370] Anna married Winfield Smith in 1928[371] and son Timothy married Anna Crabbe in 1931.[372] Katherine was still at home when her father died. She married William "Frank" Keefe on 27 September 1937 in Northampton.[373]

I do not know if Jane and Mary Ann were still in contact with one another when Timothy died, but it seems unlikely. According to Peg Leitl, Mary Ann had few positive words for Jane. She noted that when Jane's name was mentioned, Mary Ann's response was: "Don't bother with her!"[374]

Certainly, this was one of the most challenging periods for Mary Ann who was struggling to reassemble her life in the aftermath of the repossession of her home and numerous personal losses. Nathalie and William, who had been living with her, were uprooted, as well. However, by the time Home Owners' Loan executed the final papers to take back the house, Nathalie and William were already situated in Hartford.[375]

The foreclosure of the Clark home was a sad conclusion to Mary Ann's long battle with financial instability.

At some point, Mary Ann moved into Wilbur and Mae's apartment on Middle Street in Florence. The Cleary's apartment was a small space; one half of a duplex or double house as they were called in those days. It is not clear, what year she moved into the Cleary household. She may have lived with one of the other children before she took up residence with Mae in Florence.

I cannot imagine where Mae and Wilbur found space to accommodate her with five children already living under the same roof. The house was old and like most old homes, the rooms were small. The first floor consisted of a foyer, living room, an eat-in kitchen with a pantry and a bedroom that Wilbur and Mae shared. Mary Ann's space was one of two bedrooms located on the second floor overlooking the street.

I do not know what the sleeping arrangements were with just three small bedrooms to accommodate eight people. However, Mae's daughter Anne said that she shared the bedroom with Mary Ann when she was growing up. My brother and I also shared the room with Mary Ann during our extended visits with Wilbur and Mae in the nineteen-fifties.

Mary Ann's financial woes could not have come at a worse time. Mae told me that even though Wilbur continued to work in the cutlery, they "went without." They even resorted to picking berries in the summer to help support the family. Many years later, while looking through old pictures with her, she pointed to her tattered shoes in a Depression era photo and commented on how poor they were.

John and Ruth faced numerous challenges in this period, as well. A memoir entitled *Growing Up in the Great Depression* (1987), written by Cousin Jack Clark prior to his death in 1988 is an account of the hardships faced by his father (John G. Clark) and mother during the Depression.[376]

Jack's description of his parent's circumstances prior to the Depression paints a picture of an upwardly mobile couple. Recently married and without children, John owned an insurance company. Ruth was employed as a bank teller. However, insurance was considered a luxury in that period and soon after the Depression struck,

John was forced to close his company. Cousin Jack's arrival in the spring of 1930, ended his mother's job and the family was broke.[377]

This was a period when people called upon all of their skills, knowledge and creativity to survive. With a child to support and few employment prospects, the family moved to a cheaper apartment. John managed to borrow $100 to buy a truck, which he used to peddle fresh farm vegetables through the neighborhoods of Northampton.[378] It would seem their life changed almost overnight.

By 1933, John had obtained work at a local textile mill in Easthampton, but because of the decline in manufacturing, he was working short shifts. During that period the family relocated to a house close to the mill that employed him. John used the time he was not working to plant a garden. He also raised rabbits to sell and he even baked bread for his family, a skill he had acquired from a former job for a bakery.[379] Jack's depiction of life during that period brought to mind Jimmy Clark's backyard farm on Riverside Drive. Again, people drew on all of their experience and skills to survive. It would seem that John drew upon the experience of a home farm to help feed his family in the worst of times.

Jack's account of family life at that time indicates they had nothing to spare. His mother later told him, that in those days, they lived on $5.00 a week.[380]

The family moved once again in 1935 to a three decker with a shared bathroom in the hallway. John was working more steadily.[381] However, the Depression and the economic challenges for ordinary working families were not over. The anguish was widespread and perceptible.

Cousin Jack wrote that while living in the three decker, he was unable to attend school for a month due to a childhood illness. Twice each week, from the front window of the apartment that overlooked the street, he watched the abject figures of men in tattered clothing, carrying large bags and pushing wheelbarrows and carts on their way to pick up food for their families from the surplus food outlet.

He noted the men were always alone and that women were never seen with them.[382]

Even as a young child, Jack was acutely aware of the economic issues that beset his family and other local families. The poignant scene of abject looking men walking to a surplus food outlet remained with him throughout his life.

The family moved once again in 1937, to a house near the Easthampton town pond. The new larger apartment had a bathroom for the exclusive use of the family. As Jack pointed out, they had a bathtub and no longer had to bath in the tin tub his mother used to wash clothes in.[383]

It would appear life for John and his family had improved. Indeed, the nation was rebounding in that period. The U.S. economy was advancing toward levels not seen since 1929.[384] Undoubtedly, John was working more hours and in turn he was earning more. Jack recalled that with the upswing in the economy, his father was able to build a chicken coop, plant a garden, and the family was even able to afford a dog again. He received birthday presents that year, as well.[385]

While economic reports in the spring of 1937 were promising, another recession was looming over the country. Jack wrote that during the summer of 1937, people realized the hard times were about to return.[386] Once again the economy fell back into a recession.[387] While there is no indication in the memoir of how the downturn affected his family, undoubtedly like other families, John and Ruth were forced to adjust to cut backs in work hours and smaller paychecks.

While Jack noted that his parents never argued, there was trouble in the household that hearkened back to John's upbringing and the environment of Bay State Village.[388] According to Ruth's niece, Janet Richer, John drank heavily during this period.[389] My research has revealed that this problem was not limited to John. The Clark siblings with the exception of Mae sometimes drank too often and excessively. However, it appears that John's problem with alcohol ended sometime after the depression. His daughter-in-law has stated that (Jack) "...did mention it to me once, shortly after we first met, that his father had a problem with alcohol. But after that nothing more was said, and I never asked questions because it did not affect me and I always found Mr. Clark to be a sober man.[390]

Even as the country continued to recover, the residual effects of the Depression persisted. However, in 1940, John and Ruth were able to purchase a farm with a loan from the Home Owners' Loan Corporation, the same lender that wrote a mortgage for Mary Ann in 1934.

Home Owners' Loan Corporation was a government sponsored lending agency, whose primary purpose was to help homeowners avoid foreclosure during the Depression.[391] Home Owners' Loan provided low interest loans, refinancing options and a more equitable repayment program than traditional lenders.[392] While it may have been the intent of the government to assist strapped homeowners through alternative loan programs, even with the help of a low interest loan, many Americans were unable to make their payments and eventually faced foreclosure. Mary Ann was one of the statistics.

The farm was a foreclosed property.[393] This was an excellent financial opportunity for the family. Most foreclosed properties are sold at a fraction of their market value. Undoubtedly, they were able to purchase the property for a very good price.

The family made economic headway with the purchase of the farm. However, years later John had regrets about his decision not to purchase the adjoining land, despite Home Owners' offer to loan him the money. To his chagrin, when the war ended, the bordering property sold at a very high price. At the dinner table one evening he stated: "That was the biggest financial mistake of my life."[394]

While John may have felt he missed an opportunity to capitalize on his investment, buying the farm was a new beginning for him. Cousin Jack wrote that the farm represented more to his father than an investment and a means to help support his family: The farm meant that his days of mill work were over.[395]

Despite John's misgivings over passing up the opportunity to buy the adjoining property, the farm served the family well. John utilized the property to grow vegetables and raise livestock, which included pigs. During World War II, John nicknamed the pigs Adolph, Taishō and Mussolini after the leaders, who participated in the war;[396] a derisive commentary on the state of world affairs.

For a short time, the family kept milking cows on the farm, but after an outbreak of mastitis, John opted to work for H.P. Hood and Sons. He remained with the company for a number of years before running for public office.[397]

In 1960, he was elected to the Massachusetts House of Representatives and the Clark's life changed due to his role as a legislator.

During that period, the house was often used for entertaining.

The farm sustained the family by providing an income in the best and the worst of times. It served all of the family's needs, from providing fresh food and entertaining local officials, to relaxing Saturday nights on the divan where John could be found watching boxing matches.

The advancements John made in his lifetime would not have been possible had he followed the course set by his father and grandfather.

John died on 26 May 1972 at the age of 70.[398] His obituary stated:

> He was a member of the state legislature from 1961 to 1968 representing the old third Hampshire District. He was a member of the Ways and Means Committee and the Committee on Cities and Towns. He was appointed by Judge Charles O'Connor as the first assistant clerk of Hampshire District Court and retired because of illness in 1968. [399]

Ruth suffered a stroke in January 1985, which was followed "by another stroke which caused her to fall into a coma, from which she never recovered."[400] She died on 27 November 1985.[401]

The Clark family's angst over the marriage was wasted. Ruth embraced the Catholic faith and near the end of her life, she converted to Catholicism.[402] Her funeral was held at St. Mary of the Assumption in Northampton.

The farm remained in the John G. Clark family until shortly after Ruth's death in 1985.[403]

I do not know how William Clark and Nellie Dobler fared in the years immediately following the Depression.

There did not appear to be a marked change in the status of the older Clark children. Leo and Margaret maintained ownership of their home and soon after the Depression, Leo found more lucrative employment at Pratt and Whitney in East Hartford, Connecticut.[404] Mae and Wilbur continued to reside in the small rental on Middle Street in Florence. When the Clearys were enumerated in the 1940 census, there were six people living in the apartment, including Mary Ann.[405] By that time, Peg was married. Roger may have been in the service during this enumeration. Ironically, the Clearys economic status improved due to another disastrous event.

When World War II (1939-1945) commenced, the International Silver Company was awarded military contracts and unlike other local cutlery shops, where lay-offs were occurring due to a shortage of steel, International Silver flourished.[406] By the end of the war, the company had cast over seven million bombs.[407] Ed Cleary clearly remembered Wilbur bringing home an inert bomb for his children to see. Ed wrote:

Factory "F" in Florence (at the end of Middle Street was converted from making silverware to making magnesium [sic] bombs. Wilbur even bought [sic] one home, inert of course. They made the bomb casings at Factory "F" but the bombs were charged with explosives elsewhere. The casings were loaded on the "Cannon Ball Xpress" train in Florence and taken somewhere else for charging and distribution to the USAAF [sic]. [408]

The military contracts meant that Wilbur was working full-time again.

While the Clearys were getting back on their feet financially and looking forward to better times, misfortune struck once again, when their twenty-two year old son Roger was drafted into the army.[409]

Even though it had been one of Wilbur's ambitions to serve during World War I, there was no joy in the Cleary household when Roger was called to serve. From all that I have been told the younger children were most affected by his absence. On many occasions, both Anne and Ed recounted how much they missed their brother when he was away in the service. Roger was a great source of joy to them. He would often take them for rides down the back roads of Northampton in his 1938 Chevrolet and treat them to ice cream. He taught Ed to fish and hunt for squirrels and he even gave him a weekly allowance. He was in many ways a second father to him. His departure left the children devastated. However, the heartbreak did not end with the war.

In February 2000, Ed forwarded a narrative to me, written as a memorial to Roger, entitled: *Revelations of Roger Cleary*. Without a doubt, Edward's narrative of what occurred in the Cleary when Roger entered the service was an experience shared by many families in Northampton and Florence during the war. Ed wrote:

> One day the mailman delivered a letter. It was addressed to Roger J. Cleary...I was too young to understand the significance of the letter. I thought he would report to the army and come home. He, Don Curtin and Don Morin left together on the same day...
>
> After the war was over, Roger came back home to stay, but he was not the same person. I was over joyed [sic] to see him. I hugged and hugged him. I told him about the beaver pond and all the other good fishing spots that I had discovered. He didn't seem to be excited about fishing anymore...A

couple of times I caught him drinking from a bottle of booze while he was fishing. Things had definitely changed.

What I didn't realize for a long time is that he had become addicted to alcohol. He and Don Morin came back home from the war but Don Curtin didn't. Don was shot down over Germany in a B-17 bomber during a raid. I don't know if that changed Roger or if he just couldn't handle the stress of it all. He never talked about it and I never asked.[410]

Though Roger survived his enlistment and returned to Florence and the family at the end of his service, his wartime experience altered his personality. Like his Uncle Leo, it has been said that Roger was never the same.

Mary Ann and Jimmy Clarks home on Riverside Drive in Bay State. The house was foreclosed in 1937. Courtesy of Suzanne and Stephanie Smith.

Wilbur, Mae and their daughter Helene during the Depression.
Mae pointed out her tattered shoes to me, when we discussed this photo.

Maud on an excursion to Thousand Islands
prior to her devastating accident.

Maud with her second husband Jack Miller in Los Angel

Peg's confirmation photo. The family referred to her as "Peggy Baum."

Mary Beckett and Nora Connors at Mary (McCarthy) Myers internment (1949). Nora (Mccarthy) Conners and Mary (McCarthy) Myers were sisters. Courtesy of Helen (Molly) Myers

At the cottage in Onset, Massachusetts.: Edward Beckett second from the left.
Besse is on his right wearing a baseball cap. Courtesy of David McElroy.

The cottage in Onset: John F.McElroy with Edward
Beckett. Courtesy of David McElroy.

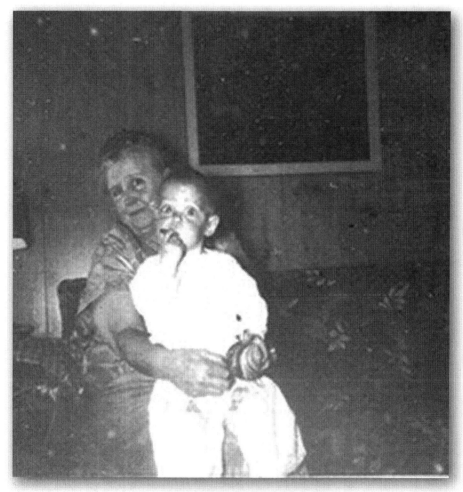

Elizabeth "Besse" (McElroy) Beckett with David
McElroy. Courtesy of David McElroy.

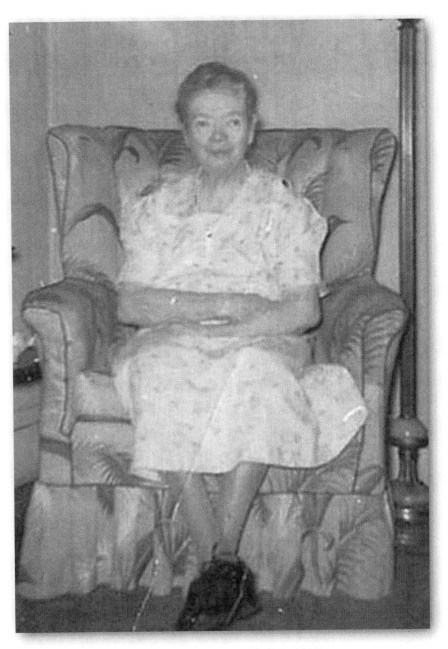

Mary Ann (Cashman) Clark (c. 1930).

William Clark (age unknown)

Leo Clark. Courtesy of Margaret (Murch) Donaghey.

Margaret (Casey) Clark with granddaughter Margaret (Murch) Donaghey (C. 1951). Courtesy of Margaret (Murch) Donaghey

Cathleen (Clark) Smith with her father (Leo Clark).
Courtesy of Cathleen (Clark) Smith.

John G. Clark c. 1960. John served as a Massachusetts state
representative for the Third Hampshire County District
(1960-1968). Courtesy of Andrienne G. Clark.

John G. Clark, Ruth Clark with Senator Ted Kennedy c. 1968.
Reproduction courtesy of W.E.B. Du Bois Library. Special Collections
and University Archives, University of Massachusetts-Amherst.

Representative John G. Clark, St. Patrick's Day parade committee, c. 1965.
Reproduction courtesy of W.E.B. Du Bois Library, Special Collections
and University Archives University of Massachusetts-Amherst.

Andrienne (Goggin) Clark and Cousin Jack Clark c. 1986. Both Jack and Andrienne contributed to this book. Courtesy of Andrienne G. Clark.

Left to right : Nathalie and William with their youngest daughter Susan
(Clark) Winchell, son-in-law Theodore Federko and Susan (Clark) Federko.

Mary Ann with Nellie (Clark) Dobler and unknown child.
Peg Leitl identified the subjects of this photo.

IX

Vicissitudes and Dotage

While space was at a premium in the Cleary household, Mary Ann had the consolation of living with her daughter Mae and her grandchildren. The extended Clark and Cashman families were nearby, as well. The Clark children did not venture far from their Northampton roots. Leo remained in Northampton. John had settled in Easthampton on the farm. Nell and William both lived in Connecticut, little more than an hour away from Northampton and Julia lived within walking distance of Mae's house. Her brother Dan Cashman resided in Portland, Connecticut.[411]

Despite the presence of her children and her surviving siblings in her life, family members have reported Mary Ann was often depressed over the absence of her youngest brother Roger, who had not communicated with the family in many years.[412] He had returned to Northampton during the twenties and spent the summer working on the construction of the Quabbin in another town. On the weekends, he stayed with Julia.[413] At some point, he boarded a train, ostensibly for the West. Initially, his communication with the family was sporadic. However, eventually all contact ceased. Mary Ann cried when she talked about him.[414] Oddly, she never spoke of Jimmy.[415]

In spite of all that she had been through, coupled with the fact that she was in her early sixties and dependent upon her daughter and son-in-law for most of her needs, Mary Ann attempted to begin a new chapter in her life. Peg Leitl told me, she began to see a widower named George Smith. Her details of the relationship were sketchy, probably because the affair did not last very long. Peg described him as tall and lean. Beyond that, she knew nothing about him. She told me that Mary Ann would often leave the house in the evening to meet him and return at about 10:00 p.m. The liaison upset the Clark children and Mary Ann ended the relationship.[416]

Throughout most of her life, Mary Ann enjoyed good health. However, in her later years she developed diabetes. Mae tried to manage her mother's condition, by restricting her intake of rich and sugary foods. From all accounts, Mary Ann viewed her daughter's efforts to keep her healthy and the diabetes in check as an attempt to control her.

Mae baked everything from scratch for her family in those days. The leftovers and sweets were always stored in the pantry in the back of the kitchen, out of sight of the family. Mary Ann managed to pilfer the leftover goodies from the pantry and hide them in her bedroom for snacking. I have been told she would sometimes share her "stash" with the Cleary children, who became co-conspirators in her efforts to sidestep Mae's supervision of her diet.[417] To the best of my knowledge, Mae never learned of Mary Ann's secret booty of sweets.

Mary Ann also enjoyed an occasional drink when out of sight of her daughter's watchful eye. When William visited, he would sometimes bring along liquor and share a drink or two with her in her room on the second floor. On several occasions, Mae discovered Mary Ann in an intoxicated state. The spectacle of her inebriated mother angered her. However, I believe Mae had a soft spot for the culprit in this story. If he was held responsible for this particular transgression, Mae's ire toward him did not last long.

It would seem there was little Mae could do to deter Mary Ann from her self-destructive activities. When she visited her granddaughter Peg and her husband Francis Leitl in Easthampton, the trio would sometimes stop at a bar on the way back to Florence for a beer and a dance.[418] It would appear that Mary Ann was so beloved by her grandchildren, they could deny her nothing, even when it was potentially dangerous to her health.

Mary Ann engaged in other diversions, as well. Her granddaughter Anne told me she would sometimes find her sitting in the chair by the window in her bedroom, smoking a cigarette in a long holder and reading detective magazines.[419] It is doubtful Mae knew about that particular diversion, either.

While Mary Ann was untraditional in many ways, she held fast to some of the Irish conventions from her youth. She still spoke some Irish around the house, rinsed her hair with tea and often dined on Colcannon, a simple dish consisting of mashed potato, and minced onions.[420]

It is unclear whether Mary Ann had a negative influence on Mae's children. However, from the information I gleaned from interviews with Anne and Peg, the Cleary grandchildren perceived Mary Ann as "nice woman," and their mother Mae, as "mean" and difficult.[421]

If Mae had any of the negative characteristics her children described, my brother Dan and I never saw that side of her. She was, for a large part of our early childhood, our mother. We respected and loved her.

The battle of wills between Mary Ann and her daughter Mae was not the only continuing dispute in the Clark family. Mary Ann's children may have concurred on the matter of their mother's relationship with George Smith, but apart from that issue, they were continually at loggerheads with one another. There was always a dispute raging between two or more of the siblings and apparently, there was no communication between some of the siblings for many years.

Cousin Jack Clark stated that he could "never recall any gathering of Grandmother's children at one time in Florence."[422] Apparently the alienation of the siblings was rooted in their responsibilities to help support their mother. Jack wrote: "Grandmother went through

Grandfather's insurance money," which was probably very little, "quickly after his death in 1927 and ended up getting relief from the city of Northampton."[423] "...it was said that Mae took the money from the city for herself."[424]

Indeed, I remember hearing the same bantering long after Mary Ann died. I believe the story was perpetuated by Mary Ann herself, who complained to family members that Mae took all of her money. I heard this story repeated many times by Mae's daughter Anne. I do not know why this spurious accusation made sense to anyone. Mae and Wilbur did not have the resources to pay for Mary Ann's care. Quite simply they needed the welfare money to support her. I am sure the money from the city was spent on her.

The animosity directed at Mae may have been rooted in the fact that all of the Clark children were responsible for contributing to part of their mother's living costs. Cousin Jack wrote: "All of her children were forced by the City of Northampton to contribute to her bills. Father had to pay just over three dollars a month."[425] Undoubtedly, the Clark siblings saw this situation as one in which they were victims, forced to pay the city that in turn handed over their hard-earned money to Mae to do as she pleased.

By 1940, the Clark children and the majority of their cousins were approaching middle age. The only surviving Clark kin of the former generation was Jane. She died on 3 November 1943.[426] Details of her funeral were reported by the *Springfield Republican* in the 6 November 1943 edition:

> "The funeral of Mrs. Jane McCarthy of 6 Pomeroy terrace [sic] was held today at the Ahearn funeral home with requiem high mass [sic] at St. Mary's church, celebrated by Rt. Rev [sic] Msgr [sic] Thomas F. Cummings. Bearers were Raymond and Edward Beckett of Providence, R.I., and George Bancroft, Leo Clark, John Nolan and Harold Myers of this city.[427]

Jane was interred with her husband Timothy at St. Mary's Cemetery in Northampton

Jane's death was followed by the unforeseen and tragic death of William "Frank" Keefe, husband of Katherine (McCarthy) in 1946.[428] William entered active duty in the Army in January 1943.[429] On 1 June 1946, the C-54 he was a passenger on, enroute to the United States, crashed into the Gulf of Salerno. The *Springfield Republican* reported:

> Mrs. Katherine (McCarthy) Keefe of 6 Pomeroy terrace, [sic] today was informed by the secretary of war that her husband, Maj. Frank Keefe of the army is "missing in flight." He is believed to be a passenger on the army transport plane out of Westover field, which crashed into the Gulf of Salerno off the Italian coast last Saturday.
>
> A native of this city and a resident of Hadley for many years before returning to Northampton to make his home, Maj. Keefe left Calcutta, India last Friday. He had a choice of making the trip home either by plane or boat, but he elected to travel by air.
>
> The boat also left India on Friday. An Associated Press report Saturday from Naples said there were only eight survivors.[430]

According to available reports, his body was never recovered. Katherine never remarried.

Regrettably, I have no further knowledge of the McCarthy family.

Upon Jane's death, all of John and Hannah's children, including William and Thomas Connors, had passed away. Mary Ann and Edward Beckett were the only surviving spouses from this generation of Clarks.[431]

The Clarks experienced numerous profound losses after Jimmy's death in 1927; however, their sorrow did not draw them closer to one another. Issues between the siblings continued to erupt. Their behavior for the most part was antagonistic, mindless and sometimes odd. Alcohol may have contributed to their conduct.

Cousin Jack recounted a bizarre incident that occurred on the family farm in Easthampton, Massachusetts during a rare period of calm in the family:

About 1949 on a Sunday afternoon on the farm a strange car drove into the yard. Mother and Father were in the yard and I came into the kitchen to see who had driven in. Before I could go outside a middle-aged woman rushed in and yelled at me, "Where is the bathroom?" I pointed to the door and she rushed in and slammed the door...she started out and then by the back door she paused and turned to me and yelled, "I don't give a — for your father and I don't give a — for you, either!" Then she rushed out and before I could reach the door the car was driving out. "Who was that?" I asked my mother as I started out of the house, and she replied, "That is your Aunt Nellie." Oddly enough, within a few years Aunt Nellie and her husband Walter Dobler became good friends of my parents.[432]

Another anecdote pertaining to a family spat which occurred between Mae and Leo at the Cleary home was reported by Ed Cleary. According to Ed when he was nine or ten years old, Leo came to the Cleary residence with a few drinks under his belt. While Mae was preparing dinner, Leo and Ed indulged in some horseplay by grabbing one anothers hands. When Leo grabbed his wrists, Ed began to cry. Ed reported:

"Mom took a cast iron frying pan from the stove, held it up in the air for Leo to see and told him to let me go...Mom moved around the stove with the frying pan upraised and yelled,

"Leo, let go of that child." Leo let me go and jumped from the chair just as Mom swung at his head with the frying pan. She missed Leo, but that was enough. He high tailed [sic] it out the front door, down the steps and out onto the front yard. I can't ever remember Leo coming to visit again."[433]

The plethora of issues and ongoing arguments between the Clark children seemed to wax and wane over the years. However, I am not sure if Mae ever reconciled with Leo. She always told me her brother Leo died in the war. Until recently, I believed that was the case.

X

I Remember...

Unfortunately, I did not have the opportunity to meet all of the Clark children. I met John and Ruth briefly on several occasions. I did not meet Nellie until I was fourteen years old. I did not know Leo or William. Since I did not spend more than a few minutes with any of the siblings, thus far I have depended on public records, letters and other family members to tell their stories.

Fortunately, I remember Mary Ann. I spent a great deal of time in the Cleary household when I was a young child. Many of my memories have faded, but I have retained some vibrant recollections of the very old woman we called "Grandmother Clark."[434]

I remember Mary Ann's room in the double house in Florence as a small, dark space. Her bed was positioned in a corner of the room. A dresser with a rounded front and glass knobs stood against the opposite wall. A plain rocking chair was placed in front of the window overlooking the street. If my recollections are correct, when we stayed with Wilbur and Mae, we slept on cots in the same room with Mary Ann.

The nicest item in the room was a piece of furniture the family always referred to as a "what-not"; a vintage Victorian étagère of ebonized cherry with mirrored back panels. The "what-not" was placed on a small wall next to the door. The piece belonged to Aunt Maud. I do not know how Mae acquired it. Later, it was used in my parents' house.[435] In 1974, Mae gave me the "what-not." To the best of my knowledge, it is the only surviving piece of furniture that belonged to Aunt Maud.

A rumor that floated through the family alleged that the étagère once belonged to a hotel owner from the South who committed suicide. I attempted to establish the provenance of this piece of furniture through associations in the John J. Miller family, but thus far, I have been unable to connect the étagère to anyone but Maud.

When I think about Mary Ann from an adult perspective, I can see that she was a creature of habit. I have a very clear memory of her sitting in a chair in the living room on Middle Street, her rosary beads entwined in her fingers, reading a black prayer book. The prayer book was so old; the thin fragile pages had separated from the binding. Saying the rosary and reading her prayers was part of her morning ritual before Mae served breakfast. Often she fell asleep in the chair.

While Mary Ann had quiet moments of prayer and reflection, she also had moments when all of her common sense went out the window. I remember standing at the top of the stairs looking on, as she sat on the edge of the bed, complaining to Mae that she could not go to bed without her face cream. She was very elderly at the time, but her voice was still strong. Mae told her it would not hurt to go to bed without it, for just one night. However, Mary Ann insisted she could not sleep without the cream. "Mae, I am not going to bed without my face cream," she insisted. The volume of her voice continued to escalate, as she insisted repeatedly, that she would not go to bed without the face cream. After several unsuccessful attempts to coax her into forgoing the cream for a night, Mae took me by the hand and led me down the stairs, where we could hear Mary Ann's shouts for face cream continue for several minutes. Eventually, her demands subsided and peace was restored.

An experience that has stayed with me all of my life occurred after dinner one evening just as Mae and Mary Ann were finishing their evening cup of tea. In those days, Mae brewed tea from loose leaves and boiling water in a teapot. I remember Mae taking me on her lap and swishing around a bit of tea that was left in the bottom of her cup. "Tell me what you see," she said, as she tilted the cup toward me. Mary Ann, who always sat at the opposite end of the table, urged me to keep looking in the bottom of the cup. What I remember seeing, was a figure of a man in the tea leaves. Mary Ann asked me if he had a mustache. (One of Mary Ann's favorite adages was: "Kissing a man without a mustache, is like eating an egg without salt.") As I looked into the bottom of the cup, I could see that indeed, he had a mustache. I do not know if what I saw was the product of my vivid imagination or the power of suggestion, but I am quite certain that is what I saw in the formation of tea leaves in the cup. They told me to keep looking. As I continued to stare into the tea leaves, I saw the outline of a man in a boat. I told them that the man in the boat was coming across the sea. My memory of this incident ends there. I later learned from interviews with Cashman descendants that reading tea leaves was popular among female family members. I never forgot that evening at the dinner table on Middle Street. Years later, I married George Banas, a man with a mustache, who had served in the U.S. Coast Guard and spent many days at sea.

Mary Ann, Elizabeth Anne Banas and Mae in the kitchen in
the double house (duplex) on Middle Street. (1953).

Mary Ann as I remember her (c. 1953).

XI

At the End of the Day

I remember visiting Mae on a cold dreary day, and even though I was quite young, I knew something was wrong. There was talk that Grandmother Clark was ill. I knew that she was not at home. I do not remember seeing her again.

Decades later, Peg Leitl told me Mary Ann fell and that Mae did not feel she could adequately care for her. Apparently, that pivotal event convinced the family to have her admitted to a nursing home in Ashfield. Apart from the fall, Mary Ann was spending more time sleeping and needed physical assistance to perform normal daily activities. I do not know what precipitated her rapid decline.[436] However, by then she was an octogenarian. It is likely her deterioration was due to the effects of aging.

Mae and Wilbur were empty nesters during this period. Ed had joined the Air Force and the other children were married with families. Still, this was an inordinately difficult period for them. Mary Ann's issues notwithstanding, they were dealing with larger more complex problems within their immediate family; a daughter's nasty divorce, a family member who had been committed to a psychiatric ward, and a son-in-law on trial for arson.[437] It was chaos. The constant strain sent Mae to the hospital for stress-related health issues for several days[438] However, she rebounded quickly and my brother and I returned to the double house, where we spent days and sometimes weeks with our grandparents.

Mary Ann's health did not improve in the nursing home. When it became clear that she was near death in early March 1955, the Clark children adopted a cooperative attitude and kept vigil over their mother.

The details of what occurred within the family in the days prior to and after Mary Ann's death would be lost in the ethers were it not for letters written by John G. and Ruth Clark to Cousin Jack, who was serving in the Air Force during that period.[439] I am sure they never dreamed the letters they dashed off to one another on a daily basis would someday be published. Even though, the letters pertain to Mary Ann's final days, her death, funeral and the family during this period, the natural attributes that won John a seat in the Massachusetts House of Representatives are apparent in his writings. While imperfect in form, the sentiments and emotions conveyed in the following excerpts from the letters are crisp and clear.

John G. Clark to Jack Clark :

6 March 1955

Today was the day your Paw was going to play diplomat and get the Clark clan back on good terms. But I must admit failure. The jell don't jell. As Mom has told you, Gram had a bad week-while there is a possibility she might hold out for a little while I really think time has about run out. Uncle Walter was here yesterday and went up to Ashfield-went with Mae and Wilbur. Then today Nell is here and I thought if Uncle Leo and Auntie Mae went up with us I would have things pretty well patched up before things happened, but I guess not. Well, you can make up your mind if Gram does go. I will read the riot act and see that everyone acts with the dignity and respectability they should.[440]

Ruth (Miller) Clark to Cousin Jack:

6 March 1955

After dinner we went to Ashfield. Found Grandmother quite a bit better — at least that is what they told us. She has no more temperature and they said she had taken a little food today. She was asleep most of the time we were there. So we didn't stay too long. When she was awake she didn't really know us. Coming through Florence we stopped and reported to Aunt Julia. Didn't stay there long — She was just getting over bronchitis and we didn't want to tire her.[441]

The Cashmans and the Clarks were unaware, as they focused on Mary Ann, that hundreds of miles away, Roger Cashman, their long lost, beloved uncle and brother, was gravely ill in a veteran's hospital in Reno, Nevada.[442]

Since Mae was listed in his military file as the next of kin. The Veterans Administration attempted to notify her of his illness. A letter dated 9 March 1955, stated in part: "Your uncle, Roger James Cashman, is seriously ill with heart disease. His condition is such at the present time that his recovery is questionable, and for that reason you are urged to visit him if at all possible."[443]

Mae's address in Roger's file was incorrectly entered as Riverside Drive. The letter never reached her. Roger passed away on 10 March at 2:45 PM.[444] The Veterans Administration sent a telegram to Mae informing her of his death.[445] This communication failed to reach her, as well. Roger's body was taken to the Ross-Burke Funeral Home in Reno, Nevada, while the Veterans Administration continued to attempt to contact family members.[446] Telegrams were also dispatched to Julia and Daniel Cashman.[447] All were undeliverable.

On 15 March 1955, Ruth and John watched on, as Mary Ann drew her last breath.

Ruth wrote of her final moments in a letter to Cousin Jack:

15 March 1955

Dear Junior,

This won't be a long letter – I wrote to you this morning, but I want to get this off to you as soon as possible, Jr. Well, Jr., to-night at 5:30 Grandmother Clark passed on. Father went to work this morning, as I wrote to you, and he got home early, as John Dearborn has done his route while he was out sick, worked with him [sic]. So father got home early--about 2:30. He took a bath and had something to eat, and said he would lie down for a couple of hours---that if he dozed off and fell asleep, I should wake him at 5:00 o'clock and then call Mae and tell her we would take her to Ashfield—leave here about 5:30. Well, father had only been lying down for about five minutes when the phone rang---it was from Ashfield, and they said that Grandmother had another spell and they thought we should get up there right away. We got up there shortly before 5:00 o'clock and at 5:30 the end came. Grandmother died very peacefully—just seemed to be asleep and grew fainter and fainter, until she just stopped breathing. We are all glad that it is over, as the longer the time went on, the more pitiful she became, and certainly she is much better off than she has been for a long time.

We came on down--stopped and told Aunt Julia and then came home. Brought Mae over here as Wilbur had to go to Meriden, Conn. today. We had a little lunch, as father cannot go too long without eating, [sic] and then he did some telephoning to notify the relations in Hartford and around here, got in touch with the undertaker and had to go to Florence to meet with him at ten o'clock to make arrangements and Father and I have just come home...[448]

Mary Ann passed away, five days after her beloved brother Roger. Despite continuous attempts on the part of the Veterans Administration, they were unable to contact family members to inform them of his death. The family began preparations for Mary Ann's funeral unaware that the unclaimed body of their uncle lay in a funeral home in Nevada.

Ruth to Cousin Jack:

17 March 1955

It was afternoon time by the time we got home, and by the time we were ready to sit down to dinner Bill Clark and Nathalie and Nellie came in. they had a cup of coffee and then they all rushed over to Florence to meet Mae and pick out a coffin and dress, etc. for Grandmother. [sic] I preferred to stay at home, as really, I was an in-law or an out-law, I don't know which, and I really didn't want them to think I was sticking my 50cs in where it wasn't appreciated. They got back here about 5:00 o'clock, and then we had supper and about 7:00 went to the funeral. They said they were going to get an orchid colored dress for Grandmother, so after they left the house in the afternoon I called up the Clark Street florists and ordered the nicest orchid I could get—told them it was to be worn on an orchid colored dress, and told them to use their own judgment on the color and told them to put on it, "To Grandmother from A/1C John P. Clark.) When we got over there, Jr., I was very pleased, and Father was too— it was perfect on the xxxxx [sic] dress. Everyone remarked about it Jr. The family got a piece—what they call a blanket for over the casket, and that was very beautiful too—made of gladioli and carnations.[449]

Ruth to Cousin Jack:

18 March 1955

Dear Jackie:

It is late but this is the first chance I have had to write to-day. Got a letter off yesterday morning and will now attempt to go on from there. Yesterday afternoon and last night we waked Grandmother. Guess I told you that I got an orchid for Grandmother from you. It was very pretty Jr., and completed everything. The dress was orchid— a pinkish shade and the flower just a shade darker and it looked as if it was just made for Grandmother. There were a large number of people at the funeral home coming and going all day and all evening and it was midnight before we got home. We had Bill and Nathalie Clark and their four boys here with us over night [sic]. Quite a houseful! Nellie stayed at Peggy Leitl's and Walter was very swell and went to Hotel Northampton for the night. We expected them to be here, but that is how it ended up for all. Bill and Nat had our bed-the youngest boy slept in yours, another in your study and the two oldest slept in the bed in the front room...[450]

John G. to Cousin Jack:

March 19, 1955

Dear Jr.,

When I say I haven't had time to write this week you can well believe me. Have had so many parts to play I don't know which one to try to describe first. Manager, business manager, judge diplomat and not least host. There were so many feuds going on I couldn't keep them all straight in my mind.

I know that Mom has told you how Gramma died quiet and peaceful. That was a great relief to me as I don't believe I could have watched a hard struggle as sometimes happens. It is best for Gram and all concerned, certainly it has been a long time since she enjoyed living.

I am sorry that you could not have been here. I would like to have you seen Gram laid out. She reminded me as I remembered her as a little boy.[451]

Mary Ann was buried in St. Mary's Cemetery next to Jimmy. To the best of my knowledge, it was the last time Clarks stood together as a family.

Over the course of the following two weeks the VA continued to send telegrams in an attempt to notify the family of Roger's death. Incredibly, all of the telegrams were undeliverable.

On 23 March 1955, Roger Cashman's remains were shipped to the Veterans Administration Center in West Los Angeles, California for burial in the National Cemetery.[452] Upon his interment, the VA closed the case.

Little more than two years after Mary Ann and Roger passed, Daniel Cashman succumbed in Portland, Connecticut, leaving Julia as the sole surviving child of Cornelius and Bridget Cashman[453]

Over the years, Julia often mentioned Roger. Time after time, her husband John suggested that they call the Veterans Administration to inquire about his whereabouts. Julia, always adamant that he would walk through the door any minute, refused and the circumstances of her long lost brother remained buried in a file at the Veteran's Administration for nearly a half century.[454]

By the time I located Roger's military pension file in 2003, nearly everyone who knew him had passed away. However, for Peg Leitl, there was closure. She loved Roger very much and over the years, like the rest of the family, she wondered what had happened to him. I believe she found comfort in the knowledge that he died of natural causes and received a proper burial.

Brothers, Kin, Mysteries and More

XII

The Hard Luck Brothers

When I began to assemble and evaluate the documents I gathered pertaining to William and Thomas Conners, it became clear that their lives were always a struggle. While I am sure they experienced some happy occasions in their lives and uninterrupted periods of peace, their lives were always difficult. The problems and the tragedies that befell them were not by their own accord.

William, the eldest of the two surviving children from Hannah's marriage to Michael Conners, appears in the enumeration of 1870, as an eleven-year-old cutlery worker.[455] However, he may have been working much earlier.

Cutleries were an unhealthy, dark and dirty environment. The air quality was poor due to contamination from metal dust that flew off the machines and hung in the air.

It was common during this period to find children working under arduous conditions. William was one of hundreds of thousands of youth who lived out their childhood in cutleries and mills with little time to grow and learn.

Apart from the additional income child laborers brought to their families, children were cheap labor, more manageable and less likely to incite a strike, all of which made them ideal employees to owners of manufacturing plants. [456]

A child labor law was passed in 1836, which provided some protection for working children.[457] The law required that children attend school at least three months out of the year and stipulated a maximum ten hour work day.[458] The 1870 census entry indicates that William's school requirement was being met. Even so, I am quite certain that William received very little formal education. The deed and the probation documents pertaining to Hannah's estate show that he signed with an (x).[459] The mark (x), a substitution for a signature, is indicative of an illiterate or handicap individual. It is noteworthy that Hannah and the other children were able to read and write. It appears that William had fewer advantages than his younger siblings.

Very little is known about William apart from what can be gleaned from the census records.

When the Clarks relocated to Northampton in 1882, William was twenty-four years old. By then, he had been working in cutleries for more than half of his life. While Northampton may have been a new beginning for Hannah and John, there was little change in William's life. He found employment at Clement Manufacturing and continued the daily grind in the cutlery shop.[460]

The 1900 census found him living with his brother Thomas and his family on Mill Street.[461] However, sometime between 1900 and 1901, he left Northampton and relocated to Shelburne Falls.[462]

William died 12 April 1901.[463] His death record indicates he was still employed as a cutler when he passed, probably at Lamson & Goodnow.[464] The cause of death was noted in the state registry as tuberculosis.[465] William never married. He is interred with John, Hannah and Jennie Doyle at St. Mary's Cemetery in Northampton.

Life for Thomas Conners was equally as challenging. It is unclear when Thomas Conners work life began. However, like the other men in the Clark household, he was employed by cutleries for most of his life. The 1901 city directory noted that he was employed by the E.E. Wood cutlery and subsequent directories for the years 1902-1907 noted that he was employed by William A. Rogers, a manufacturer of flatware[466] Earlier recordings in the censuses reported the same occupation.

Thomas was nearing the end of his third decade of life, when he married Nora McCarthy, a sister of Mary (McCarthy) Myers, who had married his cousin Michael Myers.[467] Nora was an Irish immigrant from Killarney.[468] There is no record of the Conners-McCarthy marriage on file at the City Clerk's office in Northampton. However, they were enumerated in the same household in the federal census of 1900.[469]

Thomas and Nora had two children: Nora, born 30 November 1899,[470] and James F., born, 4 February 1904.[471] Both children died at young ages. James passed on 19 November 1906, due to multiple sarcomas (cancer) at the age of two years, ten months; seven weeks after the diagnosis.[472]

Nora, the elder of the two children, died of rheumatism on 11 September 1907 at age eight.[473] Apparently, rheumatism is an outdated medical term that was commonly used to describe symptoms of arthritic conditions.[474]

Undoubtedly, it was the deaths of the children, that drove Thomas and Nora to leave Bay State. Not long after daughter Nora's death, the couple relocated to Hardwick, Vermont.[475] The 1909 city directory erroneously noted Thomas was removed to New Hampshire.[476]

The couple was enumerated in Hardwick, Vermont in the 1910 census taking. [477] Unfortunately, the image for Thomases' entry in the 1910 enumeration is nearly illegible. However, what little can be deciphered from the record noted that he was a "manager." Nora's entry stated she was employed by a hotel, probably the Hardwick Inn.[478] The couple resided on Main Street. Judging by the subsequent entries which recorded many names at the same residence, the couple lived in a boarding house. This was not an unusual living arrangement in the early nineteen hundreds. Many boarding houses provided meals, in addition to furnished rooms. Single people often lived in these types of accommodations, which were similar to hotels.

The Conners did not remain in Hardwick. The 1920 census found the couple living on Farmington Avenue in Farmington, Connecticut in the Elm Tree Inn,[479] where Thomas was employed as a "servant."[480] While he was identified as a "servant," his position was probably similar to a valet. Entries at the same address revealed boarders, servants and maids resided at the Inn.[481]

Nora was recorded as a "boarder," and her trade was entered as "maid."[482] It would appear that she was employed by the Elm Tree Inn, as well.

At some point, the couple returned to Northampton, where Thomas passed away on 16 November 1922.[483] He died of cancer of the omentum and retro pectoral gland.[484] The *Springfield Republican* reported his death: "Thomas F. Connors [sic] died today at the Cooley Dickinson Hospital. He leaves a widow, two sisters, Mrs. Edward Beckett of Providence, R.I., and Mrs. T.A. McCarthy of this city, and a half-brother, James Clark of Bay State."[485]

Thomas was the only male raised in John and Hannah's household who worked in a business apart from the manufacturing of cutlery, albeit as a "servant."

Nora was found in the 1930 enumeration of Hartford, Connecticut. During that enumeration she was employed as a scrub woman at a hotel.[486] She returned to Northampton where she died 9 August 1952 at the home of George Myers on Bright Street in Northampton.[487]

Her obituary stated :

"Mrs. Nora (McCarthy) Connors [sic] died today at the home of her nephew, George Myers of 18 Bright St., after a long illness. Born in Ireland the daughter of Michael and Mary (Callahan) McCarthy, she was employed for years at the Bond Hotel in Hartford until her retirement several years ago. Surviving are several nieces and nephews."[488]

Nora was buried at St. Mary's Cemetery in Northampton with Thomas and their two children.

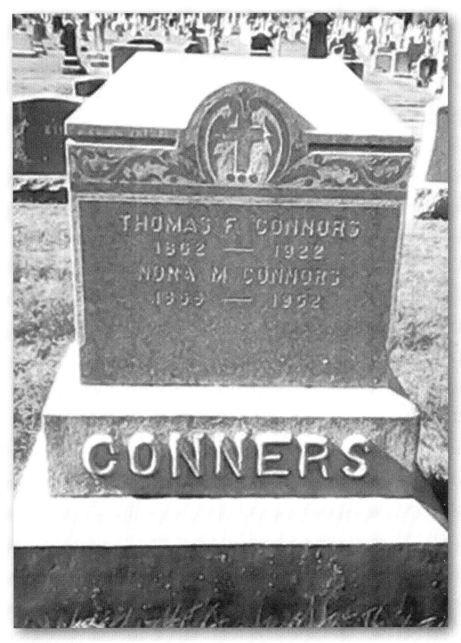

Thomas and Nora Conner's resting place at St. Mary's Cemetery, Northampton, Massachusetts. Note the alternate spellings of the name (Conners/Connors) on the headstone. Photo courtesy of George Banas.

Norah and James headstones are located in front of their parents monument. Photo courtesy of George Banas.

William Conners name is inscribed on the same side of the stone with Jennie Doyle. A subsequent chapter in this book reveals Jennie Doyle's relationship with the Clarks. Photo courtesy of George Banas.

XIII

Annie Egan: The Keeper of Records

I would be remiss if I neglected to include Annie Egan in this narrative She has a very special place in my heart. Annie was the youngest daughter of Ann (Wallace) and Patrick Myers. She was the unofficial record keeper for the Clarks and Madigans. The small black bound volume in which she pasted newspaper clippings pertaining to family members and jotted vital statistics along the margins has been an incredible resource for me. I often thank her aloud, when I am searching for a birth, death or marriage announcement. Much of the information in this book, would not have been possible without her diligence to keeping records.

Annie was born 3 September 1859 in Gill, Massachusetts.[489] She married Michael F. Egan on 20 April 1904.[490] Unfortunately, the wedding announcement that ran in the Springfield Republican disclosed little about the event: "Michael F. Egan and Miss Annie M. Myers were married at St. Mary's Church by Rev. Father Kenny." The item noted that William and Mary Purcell were the attendants.[491]

While the announcement included few details pertaining to the couple, the marriage register for the City of Northampton provided some insight into their lives. The entry stated that Michael, age 30, was employed as a cook and Annie, age 35, worked as a waitress at the time of the marriage. Their addresses (State Street and Wright Avenue) are also entered in the register book.[492]

They were married for just six years, when Michael succumbed on 10 November 1910.[493]

Annie died 24 May 1937 at the Wendall Hotel in Pittsfield, where she lived with her niece, Mary (Purcell) Campbell and her husband, Napoleon, who owned the hotel.[494]

Annie (Myers) Egan. Courtesy of Helen Myers.

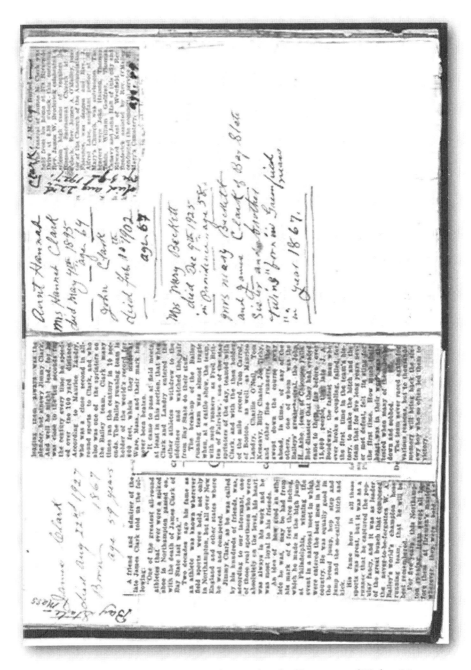

A page from Annie (Myers) Egan's scrapbook. Courtesy of Helen Myers.

XIV

The Mystery Infants: Joseph and Robert

A male child named Joseph was born to Mary Ann and Jimmy on 4 April 1904.[495] He lived for just one day. Family members I interviewed over the years had no knowledge of this child. The entry in the state registry noted the cause of death as "Strangulation-cord was twice around the child's neck."[496] It is noted in both the local certificate and the state register that a contributing cause was a "difficult labor."[497]

Both certificates state that Joseph is buried in St. Mary's Cemetery.[498] However, there is no marked grave for Joseph nor is there a record on file for his burial at the cemetery.

I met with the former superintendent of St. Mary's Cemetery Dennis Livieratos in the summer of 2013 in an attempt to establish where Joseph was buried. Through his work, Mr. Livieratos has acquired immense knowledge of the history of the cemetery. He is familiar with the cultural traditions of the early ethnic groups who lived in Northampton and buried their loved ones in the cemetery.

According to Mr. Livieratos, it was not unusual among the Irish to offer a cemetery lot to a friend when they had no place to bury a loved one.

Since the cemetery lot where Mary Ann and Jimmy are interred, was not purchased until Jimmy's death in 1927, it is clear that Joseph is not buried with them. However, there was additional space in the lots where John and Hannah were buried. It is feasible that Jimmy took it upon himself to bury Joseph with is grandparents. If that was the case, he did not report the burial to the cemetery. However, Jimmy provided the information pertaining to the child's death to the City Clerk's office in Northampton. It is possible, but not probable, the cemetery neglected to note the burial. Joseph's resting place remains a mystery. It is unlikely we will ever know where he is buried.

The story of the second infant begins with the death of Mae (Clark) Cleary. When Mae passed away in 1993, the Clark plot was opened to receive her casket. [499] To the dismay of the family, the body of an infant was unearthed on the site. Family members were stymied as to the identification of this child. However, the incident was quickly forgotten and to the best of my knowledge, no one made an inquiry to the management of the cemetery regarding the discovery of the body.

The mystery of the unnamed infant was solved years later, when James Bills shared a crushingly sad account of a baby born to William and Nathalie that died shortly after birth.[500]

During the depression, William Clark's wife Nathalie gave birth to a male infant named Robert. The child died two months later in May 1938.[501] The death occurred during the Depression; at a time, when William had few resources. We will never know what transpired in 1938; however Walter Dobler, along with his wife Nellie, drove Nathalie and William with the baby's casket from Hartford, Connecticut for burial in St. Mary's Cemetery. The child was interred with Jimmy in the lot Mary Ann purchased in 1927.

It is unknown whether Mary Ann knew of the plan to bury Robert with his grandfather. However, it is likely she had knowledge of the burial, since she is listed on the cemetery record as the owner of the lots. [502] It is likely the cemetery received Mary Ann's permission before the burial was allowed.

However, family members had no knowledge of Robert's birth or death. This may have been due to the fact, that many family members were estranged during this period.

XV

Who Was Jennie Doyle?

I am sure that visitors to Hannah and John Clark's gravesite at St. Mary's Cemetery in Northampton have noted an inscription for Jennie Doyle on the headstone and wondered as I did: Who is Jennie Doyle?

My first thought was that she was kin to the Clarks or Madigans. However, her name never appeared among the vital statistics I compiled. To the best of my knowledge, the Doyle surname did not have a connection to either family.

After some preliminary research, I learned that indeed, there is a connection between Jennie Doyle and the Clarks, albeit a distant non-blood relationship. The explanation is simple to a degree. Jennie Doyle's daughter Marie married John P. McCarthy, son of Jane and Timothy McCarthy.[503] Jennie Doyle was John P. McCarthy's mother-in-law. Apparently, John opted to use one of the available lots owned by the Clark family as a resting place for his mother-in-law.

According to the 1930 enumeration, Jennie Doyle was a widow employed as an assistant cook at a college dormitory. She was enumerated in the household of (son-in-law) John McCarthy. At the time of the enumeration, the McCarthys were living in a rental on East Street.[504]

I found it peculiar that John McCarthy would bury his mother-in-law with his grandparents. This led me to wonder if Jennie Doyle knew the Clark family. Census research showed that Jennie was a Canadian immigrant. In 1910, she and her husband Nicholas Doyle were living in Montague, Massachusetts.[505] Further research in the censuses showed that the Doyles were residing on Riverside Drive in Bay State Village during the 1920 enumeration. It is likely they knew the Clark family. [506] Mae and Wilbur lived just two houses away from Jennie and Nicholas. Jimmy and Mary Ann were also living nearby on Riverside Drive. However, Hannah and John had passed away many years prior to the Doyles relocation to Riverside Drive. It is unlikely Jennie knew either of them.

I felt that I did not resolve the question of why Jennie Doyle was buried with Hannah and John and I continued my research in newspaper archives hoping to connect her to the Clarks; perhaps through a former marriage. I located an obituary, which stated that on 24 April 1926, "Napoleon Campbell of Riverside passed away un-expectedly."[507] Jennie Doyle's name appeared among surviving family members. The item noted she was Napoleon Campbell's sister.[508] This relationship confounded me.

In 1913, Margaret (Myers) Purcell's daughter Mary married a gentleman named Napoleon Campbell.[509] However, as I began re-searching vital records, it became clear that Mary's husband was not Jennie Doyle's brother. Mary's husband, also Napoleon Campbell was the owner of the Wendall Hotel in Greenfield and at the time of the 1930 enumeration he was still living.[510] I was not able to find a familial connection between the two men, though it seems likely they were related.

I am sure there is a reasonable explanation for Jennie Doyle's burial with Hannah, John and William Conners. Perhaps in the future a McCarthy family member or Doyle family member will come forward and provide that information.

This anecdote hearkens back to my conversation with Dennis Livieratos, who noted that it was not unusual for the Irish to offer a space in the family plot to a friend who did not have a place to bury a loved one. Jennie Doyle was after all, John McCarthy's mother-in-law. She was more than a friend to John and Marie McCarthy; she was family. One possible and very simple explanation is: practicality. They had no place to bury Jennie. They knew space was available in the Clark lot and they opted to use the space to bury their loved one. At this time, there is no better explanation.

Parting Thoughts

"...there is nothing new under the sun."

While researching and writing about the lives of family members, many of whom passed from this world more than a century ago, I came to the realization that the challenges earlier generations of the Clarks faced, were not dissimilar to the challenges of this generation.

The world we inhabit today shows little semblance to their world and way of life, however our generation, like past generations of our family, have faced the same economic and personal challenges of former generations. Like those that walked before us, we suffer pain, grieve the loss of loved ones and experience moments of joy and peace.

Technology changes, styles change and attitudes change, but the human spirit is immutable.

As the years pass and my life experiences grow, I am drawn back to the truths of the Bible. When I think about family history and the people who have come and gone, I often refer to Ecclesiastics 1:9-11:

> What has been will be again. What has been done will be done again; there is nothing new under the sun.
> Is there anything of which one can say, "Look! This is something new"?

It was here already, long ago;
It was here before our time.
There is no remembrance of men of old, and even those who
are yet to come will not be remembered by those who follow.

Tempus fugit!

End Notes

1   John Clark, Primary and Final Declaration (1876), Alien Nat'l vol. 1:544, Greenfield, Massachusetts Supreme Judicial Court.

2   Ibid.

3   U.S. Social Security Death Index," database, *GenealogyBank* (http://www. genealogybank.com : accessed 20 Aug 2013), entry for John P. Clark, no. 029-28-4703. John P. was the son of Representative John G. Clark and Ruth (Miller) Clark of Easthampton, Massachusetts. John was known as "Jack."

4   John Paul Clark, "Clark Family Chronicles," p. 4; box 1:81; John G. Clark Collection, Special Collections and University Archives, W.E.B. Du Bois Library, University of Massachusetts, Amherst. Red spiral bound notebook containing a handwritten, unfinished draft entitled the "The Clark Chronicles," a collection of family traditions and anecdotes pertaining to the Clark family.

5   Cathleen (Clark) Smith [ADDRESS FOR PRIVATE USE,] Hadley, Massachusetts, interview by Elizabeth Banas, 23 October 2013; notes privately held by Banas, [ADDRESS FOR PRIVATE USE,] Belchertown, Massachusetts. Cathleen is the daughter of Leo Clark.

6   John Ennis, descendant of Mary (Clark) Beckett, ([ADDRESS FOR PRIVATE USE,] Cranston, Rhode Island, interview by Elizabeth Banas, 6 September 2013; notes privately held by Banas, [ADDRESS FOR PRIVATE USE,] Belchertown, Massachusetts, 2013.

7   Unidentified photograph, ca. 1861; digital image ca. 2008, privately held by James Bills, [ADDRESS FOR PRIVATE USE,] East Hartford, Connecticut, 2008. The author was unable to obtain permission to use this photograph.

8 Cathleen (Clark) Smith, interview, 22 November 2013. Mae and William were siblings and grandchildren of John Clark.

9 James Bills, E. Hartford, Connecticut [E-ADDRESS FOR PRIVATE USE,] to Elizabeth Banas, email, 5 October 2012, "A photo, a question and stuff," John Clark Family, John Clark, research files; privately held by Elizabeth Banas [(E-ADDRESS) & STREET ADDRESS FOR PRIVATE USE,] Belchertown, Massachusetts. James Bills is a nephew of the Clark brothers.

10 Hampshire County, Massachusetts, marriage certificate no. 134 (1866), Conners-Clark; City Clerk's Office, Northampton. Greenfield, Massachusetts, Superior Court, Alien Nat'l vol. 1:544, Primary and Final Declaration by John Clark, August Term 1876; Supreme Judicial Court, Boston.

11 Dr. Chris O'Mahoney, Manager/Research Officer, Limerick Archives, "MADIGAN OF SHANAGOLDEN," n.p., report to Helen Myers, [ADDRESS FOR PRIVATE USE,] North Hatfield, Massachusetts, 14 June 1989; photocopy held by Elizabeth Banas, [ADDRESS FOR PRIVATE USE], Belchertown, Massachusetts.

12 Ibid.

13 Bessie Arena (secretary to Father Madigan), Clarksburg, California [(EMAIL ADDRESS FOR PRIVATE USE),] to Elizabeth Banas, email, 27 July 2011, "Madigan Descendant;" Madigan family files, Hannah Madigan; privately held by Banas, [(E-ADDRESS) AND STREET ADDRESS FOR PRIVATE USE,] Belchertown, Massachusetts.

14 Dr. Chris O'Mahoney, "MADIGAN OF SHANAGOLDEN." Arena to Banas, e-mail, 27 July 2011.

15 Dr. Chris O'Mahoney, "MADIGAN OF SHANAGOLDEN."

16   Ibid.

17   Registry of Vital Records and Statistics, "Massachusetts Deaths, 1841-1915," index and images, *FamilySearch* (http://www.familysearch.org : accessed 27 July 2011), 1897, p. 39, no. 236, Ann Wallace Myers; FHL microfilm 961,522; originals held by the Massachusetts State Archives, Boston.

18   Annie (Myers) Egan, "Scrapbook," Myers Family Collection; privately held by Helen Myers, [ADDRESS FOR PRIVATE USE,] North Hatfield, MA, 2009. Book with newspaper clippings, obituaries, news articles, handwritten notes and recordings of births, marriages and deaths.

19   Annie (Myers) Egan, "Scrapbook," Myers Family Collection; page with handwritten notations of births, marriages and deaths.

20   "Massachusetts Marriages, 1695-1910," database, *FamilySearch* (http://www.familysearch.org. : accessed 26 Mar 2014), index entry for Patrick Myers and Ann Madigan, married 3 November 1852, Greenfield, Franklin County, Massachusetts; FHL microfilm 1,887,525. Patrick immigrated from Ballybricken (Limerick), Ireland.

21   "Massachusetts Marriages, 1695-1910," database, *FamilySearch* (http://www.familysearch.org : accessed 25 July 2011), index entry for Michael O'Connor and Hanora Madigan, married 10 December 1852, Greenfield, Franklin County, Massachusetts; FHL microfilm 1,887,525. Michael was born in Ireland.

22   1855 Massachusetts state census, Franklin County, population schedule, Deerfield, p. 24, dwelling 164, family 190, Michael Conners household; digital images, *FamilySearch* (http://www.familysearch.org : accessed 17 Aug 2011); FHL microfilm 953,947; originals held by the Massachusetts State Archives, Boston. The family was enumerated as "Conners" in this census taking.

23   1855 Massachusetts state census, Franklin Co., pop. sch., Deerfield, p. 24, dwell. 164, fam. 190, Michael Conners household.

24   Registry of Vital Records and Statistics, "Massachusetts Births, 1841-1915," index and images, *FamilySearch* (http://www.familysearch.org : accessed 27 July 2011) 1853, p. 39, no. 236, John Conners; FHL microfilm 1,420,836; originals held by the Massachusetts State Archives, Boston.

25   Franklin County, Massachusetts, death certificate no. 28 (1855), John Conners, Town Clerk's Office, Deerfield.

26   Registry of Vital Records and Statistics, "Massachusetts Births, 1841-1915," index and images, *FamilySearch* (http://www.familysearch.org : accessed 27 July 2011), 1854, p. 263, no. 38, Michael Conners; FHL microfilm 4,341,205; originals held by the Massachusetts State Archives, Boston.

27   Franklin County, Massachusetts, death certificate no. 49 (1857), Michael Conners Jr., Town Clerk's Office, Deerfield.

28   Registry of Vital Records and Statistics, "Massachusetts Births, 1841-1915," index and images, *FamilySearch* (http://www.familysearch.org : accessed 27 July 2011), 1856, p. 289, no. 70, Daniel Conners; FHL microfilm 1,428,234; originals held by the Massachusetts State Archives, Boston.

29   Franklin County, Massachusetts, death certificate no. 54 (1856), Daniel Conners, Town Clerk's Office, Deerfield.

30   Registry of Vital Records and Statistics, "Massachusetts Births, 1841-1915," index and images, *FamilySearch* (http://www.familysearch.org: accessed 27 July 2011), 1858, p. 301, no. 80, William Conners; FHL microfilm 1,420,936; originals held by the Massachusetts State Archives, Boston.

31   Registry of Vital Records and Statistics, "Massachusetts Births, 1841-1915," index and images, *FamilySearch* (http://www.familysearch.org : accessed 27 July 2011), 1860, p. 348, no. 18, Thomas Conners; FHL microfilm 1,428,238; originals held by the Massachusetts State Archives, Boston.

32   1865 Massachusetts state census, Franklin County, population schedule, Greenfield, n.p., dwelling 280, family 334, Hannah Madigan; digital images, *FamilySearch* (http://www.familysearch.com : accessed 8 Aug 2011); FHL microfilm 0,954,563; originals held by the Massachusetts State Archives, Boston. Hannah was enumerated under her maiden name, "Hannah Madigan." Thomas and William were entered as "Thomas Conners" and "William Conners."

33   Annie (Myers) Egan, "scrapbook," Myers Family Collection.

34   Hampshire County, Massachusetts, marriage certificate no. 134 (1866), Madigan-Clark; City Clerk's Office, Northampton.

35   Ibid.

36   Ibid.

37   Ibid.

38   Ibid.

39   O'Mahoney, MADIGAN OF SHANAGOLDEN; Bessie Arena, email, 27 July 2011.

40   Elise Bernier-Feeley, Local History and Genealogy Librarian, Forbes Library, Northampton, Massachusetts [E-ADDRESS FOR PRIVATE USE] to Elizabeth Banas, e-mail, 1 Jul 2013, "Father F.I. Lynch," John Clark Family File, John Clark; privately held by Elizabeth Banas [(E-ADDRESS) &

STREET ADDRESS FOR PRIVATE USE,] Belchertown, Massachusetts. Father Lynch was born in Ireland and served at St. John's for four years.

41   Franklin County, Massachusetts, birth certificate no. 45 (1868), James Clark (twin); Town Clerk's Office, Deerfield;

42   Franklin County, Massachusetts, birth certificate no. 45 (1868), Mary R. [H.] Clark (twin); Town Clerk's Office, Deerfield. Mary's middle name was Hannah.

43   Registry of Vital Records and Statistics, "Massachusetts Births, 1841-1915," 1869, p. 297, no. 58, Jane E, Clark; index and images, *FamilySearch* (http://www.familysearch.org : accessed 23 Aug 2011), FHL microfilm 1,428,072; originals held by the Massachusetts State Archives, Boston.

44   Cheapside was annexed to Greenfield in 1896.

45   1870 U.S. census, Franklin County, Massachusetts, population schedule, Deerfield, Enumeration District (ED) Deerfield Post Office, p. 48 (penned), dwelling 318, family 385, William Conners; digital image, *Ancestry.com* (http://www.ancestry.com : accessed 4 Aug 2013); citing National Archives microfilm publication M593_615; FHL microfilm 552,114. The entry for William stated that he was employed by a cutlery.

46   1870 U.S. census, Franklin County, Massachusetts, population schedule, Deerfield Post Office, pp. 46-51 (penned), dwellings 311-340, families 377-418, John Barry-Dennis Mitchell; digital images, *Ancestry.com* (http://www.ancestry.com : accessed 26 June 2013); citing National Archives microfilm publication M593_ 615; FHL microfilm 552,114;

47   Greenfield, Massachusetts, Alien Nat'l vol. 1:544, John Clark, 1876.

48   Franklin County, Massachusetts, Deeds, 241: 309, David and Electa Hawks to Ann Murphy, 29 Feb 1864; Franklin County Registry of Deeds, Greenfield.

49   Unknown author, "Shelburne Falls," Gazette and Courier, 14 June 1875, *Publication Archive: The Franklin County Publication Archive Index* (http://www.publicationarchives.com : accessed 12 Dec 2008). Courtesy of "Stew."

50   Greenfield, Massachusetts, Alien Nat'l vol. 1:544, John Clark, 1876; Primary and Final Declaration (1876), Massachusetts Supreme Judicial Court Archives, Boston, Massachusetts.

51   Greenfield, Massachusetts, Alien Nat'l vol. 1:544, John Clark, 1876.

52   Ibid.

53   1880 U.S. census, Franklin County, Massachusetts, population schedule, Buckland, Enumeration District (ED) 244, p. 27 (penned), sheet 42-C (stamped), dwelling 256, family 312, Geo D. Crittenden; digital images, *Ancestry.com* (http://www.ancestry.com : accessed 25 Nov 2013); citing National Archives microfilm publication T9; FHL microfilm 1,254,533. Franklin County, Massachusetts, Unindexed Property, Book 342: 141, Clark to Crittenden, 22 Sept 1879; digital images, Secretary of the Commonwealth of Massachusetts, *Masslandrecords.com* (http://www.masslandrecords.com/Franklin/ : accessed 8 Oct 2011).

54   Franklin County, Massachusetts, Unindexed Property, Book 344 :39, Crittenden to Clark, 22 Sept 1879; digital images, Secretary of the Commonwealth of Massachusetts, *Masslandrecords.com* (http://www.masslandrecords.com/Franklin/ : accessed 8 Oct 2 1880).

55   Franklin County, Massachusetts, Unindexed Property, Book 366: 36, Clark to Adler, 5 Dec 1882; digital images, Secretary of the Commonwealth of Massachusetts, *Masslandrecords.com* (http://www.masslandrecords.com/Franklin/ : accessed 8 Oct 2011).

56   1880 U.S. census, Franklin County, Massachusetts, population schedule, Buckland, Enumeration District (ED) 244, p. 24-D (penned), dwelling 232,

family 280, Christian Adler; digital images, *Ancestry.com* (http://www.ancestry.com : accessed 7 May 2013); citing National Archives microfilm publication T9; FHL microfilm 1,254,533.

57   "Hampshire County-Northampton," *Springfield* (MA) *Republican*, 1 Sept 1882 p. 6, no col., digital image, *GenealogyBank* (http://www.genealogybank.com : accessed 2 Aug 2013).

58   Ibid.

59   Hampshire County, Massachusetts, Unindexed Property, Book 377: 125, Jeremiah Brown to Hannah Clark, deed, 15 Feb 1883; digital imagse, Secretary of the Commonwealth-Registry of Deeds, *Masslandrecords.com* (http://www.sec.state.ma.us/sec/rod/rodhamp/hampidx.htm : accessed 21 Aug 2011. When the Clarks purchased the property, the street address was Main Street. The street name was later changed to Riverside Drive.

60   Hampshire Co., MA, Unindexed Property, Book 377: 125, Brown to Clark deed, Feb. 1883.

61   Ibid.

62   Dave Manuel, "DaveManuel.com: Inflation Calculator," database, *Davemanuel.com* (http://www.davemanuel.com : accessed 25 Nov 2013).

63   Riverside Drive was formerly known as Main Street.

64   *Northampton and Easthampton Directory, 1883-1884* (Northampton, MA: The Price, Lee and Co., 1883), 32, entry for "Conners, Thomas"; digital images, *Ancestry.com* (http://www.ancestry.com : accessed 5 Jul 2013). Thomas Conners's address is entered in the directory as Hinkley Street (Bay State). It is noted he roomed at the Hinkley Street address.

65 *Northampton and Easthampton Directory, 1883-1884*, 32, entry for "Conners, William;" digital images, *Ancestry.com* (http://www.ancestry.com : accessed 5 Jul 2013). William's address is entered as Vernon Street (Bay State).

66 *Northampton and Easthampton Directory, 1887-1888*, (Northampton, MA: The Price and Lee Co., 1887), 38, entries for "Conners, William and Thomas"; digital images, *Ancestry.com* (http://www.ancestry.com : accessed 5 Jul 2013). The brothers probably lived with Hannah and John.

67 Registry of Vital Records and Statistics, Marriages, 1886, p. 25, no. 125, Edward J. Beckett and Mary H. Clark; from "Massachusetts Marriages, 1841-1915," digital images, *FamilySearch* (http://www.familysearch.org : accessed 22 Aug 2011), FHL microfilm 1,415,222; originals held by the Massachusetts State Archives, Boston.

68 "Bay State," *The Northampton (MA) Daily Herald*, 19 Nov 1886, n.p., col. 5; (Northampton, MA: E.C. Stone, 1885-1921), n.p.; "Northampton Daily Herald [microform]," (Oct 1, 1885)-April 11, 1921; Newspaper Collection, July-December 1886; microfilm held by the W.E.B. Du Bois Library, University of Massachusetts, Amherst.

69 Registry of Vital Records and Statistics, "Massachusetts, Births and Christenings, 1620-1988," index and images, *Ancestry.com* (http://www.an-cestry..com : accessed 27 Mar 2014), 1887, p. 93, no. 80, Kate Beckett; FHL microfilm 1,428,239; originals held by the Massachusetts State Archives, Boston. This date is inconsistent with the death register entry, which notes the date of death as 6 April 1887.

70 Ibid.

71 Registry of Vital Records and Statistics, "Massachusetts, Deaths, 1841-1915," index and images, *FamilySearch* (http://www.familysearch.org : accessed 27

Mar 2014), 1887, n.p., no. 73, Kate Beckett; FHL microfilm 960,235; originals held by the Massachusetts State Archives, Boston.

72 Ibid. The infant's birth date was calculated by way of the information in the
death registry entry.

73 Ibid. The register book also notes a permit was issued on 23 May 1906 for
removal to Providence, Rhode Island.

74 Registry of Vital Records and Statistics, "Massachusetts Births, 1841-1915,"
index and images, *FamilySearch* (http://www.familysearch.org : accessed 15
Jul 2013), 1862, p. 78, no. 143, Edward Beckett; FHL microfilm 1,420,998;
originals held by the Massachusetts State Archives, Boston;

75 Registry of Vital Records and Statistics, "Massachusetts Births, 1841-1915,"
index and images, *FamilySearch* (http://www.familysearch.org : accessed
15 Jul 2013), 1862, p. 78, no. 144, John Beckett; FHL microfilm 1,420,998;
originals held by the Massachusetts State Archives, Boston;

76 Ibid.

77 1865 Massachusetts state census, Hampshire County, population schedule,
Northampton, n.p., dwelling 1053, family 1301, Thomas Beckett household,
digital image, *FamilySearch* (familysearch.org : accessed 8 Aug 2011); FHL
microfilm 0954,566; Massachusetts State Archives, Boston.

78 Registry of Vital Records and Statistics, Marriages, "Massachusetts
Marriages, 1841-1915," index and images, *FamilySearch* (http://www.
familysearch.org : accessed 16 July 2013), 1886, p. 25, no. 125, Edward J.
Beckett and Mary H. Clark; FHL microfilm 1,415,222; originals held by the
Massachusetts State Archives, Boston; Mamie's occupation is entered in the
register book as "silk mill."

79 Registry of Vital Records and Statistics, "Massachusetts, Births, 1841-1915," index and images, *FamilySearch* (http://www.familysearch.org : accessed 16 July 2013), 1889, p. 19, no. 42, George Beckett; FHL microfilm 960,241; originals held by the Massachusetts State Archives, Boston

80 Registry of Vital Records and Statistics, "Massachusetts, Deaths, 1841-1915," index and images, *FamilySearch* (http://www.familysearch.org : accessed 16 July 2013), 1889, p. 22, no. 52, George Beckett; FHL microfilm 960,241; originals held by the Massachusetts State Archives, Boston.

81 Registry of Vital Records and Statistics, "Massachusetts, Births, 1841-1915," index and images, *FamilySearch* (http://www.familysearch.org : accessed 16 July 2013), 1891, p. 35, no. 304, Edward Beckett; FHL microfilm 1,843,693; originals held by the Massachusetts State Archives, Boston.

82 Registry of Vital records and Statistics, "Massachusetts, Births, 1841-1915," index and images, *FamilySearch* (http://www.familysearch.org : accessed 16 July 2013), 1894, p. 32, no. 79, Annie Beckett; FHL microfilm 1,651,225; originals held by the Massachusetts State Archives, Boston.

83 "Massachusetts, Births, 1841-1915," database, *FamilySearch* (http://www.familysearch.org : accessed 16 July 2013), index entry for James I. Beckett born 23 August 1896, Northampton, Hampshire County, Massachusetts; FHL microfilm 1,843,693.

84 *"Northampton and Easthampton Directory, 1887"* (Northampton, MA: The Price, Lee & Co., 1887), 23, entry for "Beckett, Edward"; digital image, *Ancestry.com* (http://www.ancestry.com : accessed 20 July 2013). Also subsequent years by the same title: (1889) 22, (1890) 23, (1891) 31, (1892) 16, (1895) 16, (1896) 16, (1898) 17. The directories record the Becketts residing on Riverside Drive, Mill Street, Hinkley Street, Union Street and River Street.

85 *Northampton and Easthampton Directory, 1898* (Northampton, MA: The Price, Lee and Co., 1898), 25, entry for "Beckett, Edward J."; digital image, *Ancestry.com* (http://www.ancestry.com : accessed 10 Jul 2013). This entry notes that Edward was removed to Providence, Rhode Island.

86 1910 U.S. census, Providence County, Rhode Island, population schedule, Providence, Enumeration District (ED) 180, sheet 21-A (penned), p. 174 (stamped), dwelling 326, family 435, Edward Beckett; digital image, *Ancestry.com* (http://www.ancestry.com : accessed 19 Aug 2013); National Archives microfilm publication T624_1442. 1915 Rhode Island state census, Providence County, population schedule, Providence, p. H, dwelling 54, family 81, Edward Beckett; digital images, *Ancestry.com* (http://www.ancestry.com : accessed 7 Oct 2013); FHL microfilm 1,375,455.

87 "Rhode Island, Births and Christenings," database, *FamilySearch* (http://www.familysearch.org : accessed 7 Aug 2013), index entry for Raymond Clark Beckett born 6 Aug 1899 in Providence, Providence County, Rhode Island; FHL microfilm 1,822,784.

88 "Rhode Island, Births and Christenings," database, *FamilySearch* (http://www.familysearch.org : accessed 7 Aug 2013), index entry for Jane Ester Beckett born 21 Apr 1901 in Providence, Providence County, Rhode Island; FHL microfilm 2,208,954.

89 Rhode Island State Death Register, death certificate, Vol. 1901: 209, Jennie Clark Beckett, Rhode Island State Archives, Providence.

90 "Rhode Island, Births and Christenings, 1600-1914," database, *FamilySearch* (http://www.familysearch.org : accessed 8 Aug 2013), index entry for Florence Agnes Beckett, born 27 March 1904 in Providence, Providence County, Rhode Island; FHL microfilm 2,208,954.

91 "Rhode Island, Births and Christenings," database, *FamilySearch* (http://www.familysearch.org : accessed 7 Aug 2013), index entry for Mary Gertrude, born 18 Feb 1906 in Providence, Providence County, Rhode Island; FHL microfilm 2,208,954.

92 "Rhode Island, Births, 1636-1930," database, *Ancestry.com* (http://www.ancestry.com : accessed 19 Aug 2013), index entry for Ruth H. Beckett, born 7 September 1910 in Rhode Island.

93 "Rhode Island Births, 1636-1930," database, *Ancestry.com* (http://www.ancestry.com : accessed 19 Aug 2013), index entry for Helen Irene Beckett, born 19 Mar 1913 in Rhode Island;

94 Providence, Rhode Island, death certificate unnumbered (1913), Helen Irene Beckett; Rhode Island State Archives, Providence. Helen was 5 months, 14 days at the time of death.

95 Providence, Rhode Island, death certificate unnumbered (1904), James Beckett; Rhode Island State Archives, Providence.

96 *The Providence Directory* (Providence, Rhode Island: Sampson & Murdock Co., 1901), 130, "Beckett, Edward J."; digital image, *Ancestry.com* (http://www.ancestry.com : accessed 28 Feb 2014); also subsequent years by the same title: (1903) 120, (1904) 141, (1906) 147, (1908-1909) 133, (1910) 134, (1911) 135, (1912) 136, (1914) 138, (1916) 138, (1918) 140, (1920) 145, (1922) 145, (1924) 147.

97 "The South-Street Fire Saturday Night," *Springfield* (MA) *Republican*, 23 August 1886, p. 5, no col.; digital image, *GenealogyBank* (http://www.genealogybank.com : accessed 14 May 2011). The Caledonian Club was organized by Scottish immigrants as a cultural and charitable organization for the benefit of the Scottish immigrant community.

98 "Northampton," *Springfield* (MA) *Republican*, 29 Aug 1887, p. 3, no col.; digital image, *GenealogyBank* (http://www.genealogybank.com : accessed 7 July 2013). The Ancient Order of the Hiberians (AOH) is an Irish-Catholic fraternal order organization.

99 Frank Zarnowski, *American Work-Sports: A History of Competitions for Cornhuskers, Lumberjacks, Firemen and Others* (Jefferson: McFarland & Company, Inc.), pp. 46-47.

100 Ibid.

101 "Hampshire County," *Springfield* (MA) *Republican*, 6 Oct. 1890, p. 5, no. col., digital image, *GenealogyBank* (http://www.genealogybank.com : accessed 7 July 2013).

102 "Here and There with T.F.F.," clipping, *Daily Hampshire* (MA) *Gazette*, 29 August 1927, p. 10, col. 4. This clipping was a gift from Andrienne Clark. Reproduction of this item courtesy of the *Daily Hampshire Gazette.*

103 Clark family tradition regarding how Jimmy and Mary Ann met. Elizabeth Banas (undated notes, privately held by Banas [ADDRESS FOR PRIVATE USE,] Belchertown, Massachusetts), as reported by Mary H. (Clark) Cleary, daughter of Mary Ann (Cashman) and James Clark. [Mary Ann told Mae this story.]

104 "U.S. City Directories, 1821-1989," database, *Ancestry.com* (http://www.ancestry.com : accessed 19 Dec 2013), entry for Cornelius Cashman; citing Northampton, Massachusetts, City Directory, 1899 (Northampton, MA: The Price & Lee Company, 1899), p. 32.

105 Hampshire County, Massachusetts, death certificate (1955), Mary A. (Cashman) Clark, City Clerk's Office, Northampton. No birth record for Mary Ann was located in Ireland. Her birth date was calculated via the data contained in the death certificate (85 years, 5 months, 16 days).

106 Fermoy District, Ireland, Marriage Register, 1865, November, no. 14, Con Cashman-Bridget McGrath; General Register Office, Dublin. The marriage certificate notes that Cornelius (Con) was a laborer and Bridget a servant.

107 Mallow Heritage Centre, "Roman Catholic Baptisms and Marriages for the Diocese of Cloyne," database, Ellen Cashman born 30 Aug 1866 in Conna, Cork, Ireland, ID 1397234. Originals held by the General Registrars Office, Dublin, Ireland. Computer print-out and data provided by the Mallow Heritage Center.

108 Mallow Heritage Centre, "Roman Catholic Baptisms and Marriages for the Diocese of Cloyne," database, Julia Cashman born 11 Nov 1870 in Conna, Cork, Ireland, ID 1397237. Originals held by the General Registrars Office, Dublin, Ireland. Computer print-out and data provided by the Mallow Heritage Center.

109 Mallow Heritage Centre, "Roman Catholic Baptisms and Marriages for the Diocese of Cloyne," database, Margaret Cashman born 22 June 1873 in Castlelyons, Cork, Ireland, ID 1897190. Originals held by the General Registrars Office, Dublin, Ireland. Computer print-out and data provided by the Mallow Heritage Center.

110 Mallow Heritage Centre, "Roman Catholic Baptisms and Marriages for the Diocese of Cloyne," database, Daniel Cashman born 11 July 1875 in Rathcomac, Cork, Ireland, ID 471461. Originals held by the General Registrars Office, Dublin, Ireland. Computer print-out and data provided by the Mallow Heritage Center.

111 Mallow Heritage Centre, "Roman Catholic Baptisms and Marriages for the Diocese of Cloyne," database, Roger Cashman born 6 July 1877 in Castlclyons, Cork, Ireland, ID 16673889. Originals held by the General Registrars Office, Dublin, Ireland. Computer print-out and data provided by the Mallow Heritage Center.

112 Mallow Heritage Centre, "Roman Catholic Baptisms and Marriages for the Diocese of Cloyne," database, Catherine Cashman, unknown birth date, ID 471462. Originals held by the General Registrars Office, Dublin, Ireland. Computer print-out and data provided by the Mallow Heritage Center.

113 New York Passengers Lists, 1820-1957, digital image, *Ancestry.com* (http://www.ancestry.com : accessed 15 June 2011), manifest Arizona, Queenstown, Ireland to Castle Garden, New York arriving 18 Sept. 1882, n.p., William Cashman; citing National Archives microfilm publication M237_457. William's entry states he was an "infant."

114 Manifest, *"Germanic,"* 30 May 1881, n.p., for Helen Cashman (age 15), digital image, *Ancestry.com* (http://www.ancestry.com : accessed 21 Dec 2010).

115 Manifest, Arizona, 18 Sept 1882, n.p., for Con Cashman (age 38), Bridget(age 38), Mary (age 14), Julia (age 11), Margaret (age 10), Daniel (age 8), Roger (age 6), William (infant), digital image, *Ancestry.com* (http//www.ancestry. com : accessed 15 Nov 2008).

116 John P. Clark, "Clark Family Chronicles," p. 8, John G. Clark Collection, Special Collections and University Archives, W.E.B. Du Bois Library, University of Massachusetts, Amherst.

117 Hampshire County, Massachusetts, marriage certificate (1895), Clark-Cashman, City Clerk's Office, Northampton. Entries in this record state that Mary Ann was 24 (silk spooler) and James was 27 (grinder).

118 "Florence," *Daily Hampshire* (MA) *Gazette*, 27 February 1895, n.p, no col., (Northampton, Mass.: H.S. Gere and Sons 1890-); *"Daily Hampshire Gazette* [microform]," January 21,1895-July 29, 1895; microfilm held by Forbes Library, Northampton, MA.

119 W.A. Bailey Running team photograph, undated, image copy, privately held by James Bills, [ADDRESS FOR PRIVATE USE,] East Hartford,

Connecticut, 2008. This image depicted Tom Keneavy wearing a W.A. Bailey uniform in the background of the photo. Keneavy was identified by comparing his image in the 26 Feb 1895, Clark-Cashman wedding photo. The author did not receive permission to reprint the photo.

120 Hampshire County, Massachusetts, birth certificate (Reg.) no. 185 (1895), Leo Ernest Clark, City Clerk's Office, Northampton.

121 Hampshire County, Massachusetts, birth certificate (Reg.) no. 166 (1898), Mary Hannah Clark, City Clerk's Office, Northampton.

122 Registry of Vital Records and Statistics, "Massachusetts Births, 1841-1915," index and images, *FamilySearch* (http://www.familysearch.org : accessed 23 Feb 2012), vol. 485, p. 253, no. illegible, Helen Catherine Clark; FHL microfilm 1,843,711; originals held by the Massachusetts State Archives, Boston

123 Registry of Vital records and Statistics, "Massachusetts Births, 1841-1915," index and images, *FamilySearch* (http://www.familysearch.org : accessed 18 Dec 2012), 1902, p. 252, no. 73, John George Clark; FHL microfilm 2,057,388; originals held by the Massachusetts State Archives, Boston.

124 Hampshire County, Massachusetts, death certificate no. 91 (1904), Joseph Clark; City Clerk's Office, Northampton.

125 Registry of Vital records and Statistics, "Massachusetts Births, 1841-1915, index and images, *FamilySearch* (http://www.familysearch.org : accessed 9 July 2013), 1905, p. 268, no. 444, William Cornelius Clark; FHL microfilm 2,057,531; originals held by the Massachusetts State Archives, Boston

126 Hampshire County, Massachusetts, death certificate (1895), Hannah (Madigan) Clark; City Clerk's Office, Northampton.

127 "BAY STATE," *Daily Hampshire* (MA) *Gazette*, 5 May 1895, n.p., col. 5; (Northampton, Mass.: H.S. Gere and Sons 1890-); "*Daily Hampshire Gazette*

[microform]," January 21,1895-July 29, 1895; microfilm held by Forbes Library, Northampton, MA.

128 "BAY STATE," *Daily Hampshire* (MA) *Gazette,* 7 May 1895, n.p., col. 3; (Northampton, Mass.: H.S. Gere and Sons 1890-); *"Daily Hampshire Gazette* [microform]," January 21,1895-July 29, 1895; microfilm held by Forbes Library, Northampton, MA.

129 Dr. Chris O'Mahoney, "MADIGAN OF SHANAGOLDEN." Hannah was born 23 October 1826.

130 Hampshire County, Massachusetts, Book 475: 177, Clark to Clark, 16 May 1895; digital image, Secretary of the Commonwealth of Massachusetts, *Masslandrecords.com* (http://www.masslandrecords.com/Franklin/ : accessed 21 Aug 2011).

131 Ibid.

132 Hampshire County, Massachusetts, Book 377: 311-312, Homestead Declaration, 16 March 1883; digital image, Secretary of the Commonwealth-Registry of Deeds, *Hampshire District Registry of Deeds* (http://www.sec. state. ma.us/rod/rodhamp/hampidx.htm : accessed 23 Aug 2013.

133 Hampshire County, Massachusetts, Book 499: 103, Jane E. Clark et al to Thomas Halpin et ux, 8 June 1897, digital image, Secretary of the Commonwealth of Massachusetts, *Masslandrecords.com* (http://www.masslandrecords.com/ Hampshire/ : accessed 22 July 2010). It is commonplace to find the actual sale price (of a property) omitted in lieu of a recording of one dollar.

134 Ibid.

135 Ibid.

136 "Massachusetts Deaths, 1841-1915," *FamilySearch*, index and images 1897, p. 39, no. 236, Ann Wallace Myers.

137 Helen Myers, great-granddaughter of Ann Myers, ([ADDRESS FOR PRIVATE USE], North Hatfield, MA), c. 2008; notes, privately held by author, ([ADDRESS FOR PRIVATE USE], Belchertown, MA), 2008.

138 Ibid.

139 "Obituary," *Northampton Daily Herald*, 17 Sept. 1897, n.p., col. 2; (Northampton, Mass.: E.C. Stone, 1885-1921); *Northampton Daily Herald* [microform]," (Oct 1, 1885)-April 11, 1921; microfilm held by Forbes Library, Northampton, MA.

140 Registry of Vital Records and Statistics, "Massachusetts, Marriages, 1841-1915," index and images, *FamilySearch* (http://www.familysearch.org : accessed 28 Aug 2013), 1887, p. 412, no. 65, Michael Myers and Mary McCarthy; imaged from FHL microfilm 1,415,223; originals held by the Massachusetts State Archives, Boston. The entry notes that Patrick and Ann (Myers) were Michael's parents. Michael was born c. 1859.

141 Registry of Vital Records and Statistics, "Massachusetts Town and Vital Records, 1620-1988," index and images, *Ancestry.com* (http:www.//ancestry.com : accessed 28 Aug 2013), 1877, p. 41, no. 29, John Purcell and Margaret Myers; FHL microfilm 1,433,037; originals held by the Massachusetts State Archives, Boston; The entry notes that Ann and Patrick Myer's were Margaret's parents.

142 Registry of Vital Records and Statistics, "Massachusetts Births, 1841-1915," index and images, *FamilySearch* (http://www.familysearch.org : accessed 22 Jan 2014), 1859, p. 305, no. 7, Anna Maria Myers; FHL microfilm 1,428,237; originals held by the Massachusetts State Archives, Boston.

143 Annie (Myers) Egan, "Scrapbook," Myers Family Collection; page with handwritten notations for Myer's birth and deaths, which includes an entry for Catherine, died 2 August 1854, 1 year and nine months old.

144 Registry of Vital Records and Statistics, "Massachusetts, Deaths, 1841-1915," index and images, *FamilySearch* (http://www.familysearch.org : accessed 27 Aug 2013), vol. 165, p. 288, no. 3, Myers; FHL microfilm 0,960,182; originals held by the Massachusetts State Archives, Boston.

145 Registry of Vital Records and Statistics, "Massachusetts Deaths, 1841-1915," index and images, *FamilySearch* (http://www.familysearch.org : accessed 17 Aug 2013), vol. 220, p. 284, no. 4, Patrick Myers; FHL microfilm 960,194; originals held by the Massachusetts State Archives, Boston

146 "Massachusetts Births, 1841-1915," database, *FamilySearch* (http://www.familysearch.org : accessed 13 Apr 2014), index entry for Timothy McCarty [McCarthy], born 18 Nov 1870 in Northampton, Hampshire County, Massachusetts; FHL microfilm 1,428,073.

147 "Massachusetts, Births, 1841-1915," database, *FamilySearch* (http://www.familysearch.org: accessed 13 Apr 2014), index entry for Mary Mccarty [McCarthy], born 18 November 1870 in Northampton, Hampshire County, Massachusetts; FHL microfilm 186,182. Mary does not appear in subsequent census takings. A death record for her was not located.

148 Ibid.

149 Northampton, Massachusetts, probate case file 13287, Johanna McCarthy (1920) will; Hampshire County Probate and Family Court, Northampton. Johanna's will noted the names her surviving children (John, Eugene, Anna and Timothy). Registry of Vital Records and Statistics, "Massachusetts Deaths, 1841-1915," index and images, *FamilySearch* (http://www.familyse-arch.org : accessed 14 May 2014), p. 207 (reg.) no. 248 (1907), Catherine

(McCarthy) Bishop; FHL microfilm 2,217,349; originals held by the Massachusetts State Archives, Boston. Registry of Vital records and Statistics, "Massachusetts Death Records, 1841-1915," *Ancestry.com*, database and images, death certificate, p. 59, (reg.) no. 100 (1907), Patrick McCarthy Jr.; citing *Massachusetts Vital Records 1840-1911*; New England Historic Genealogical Society; originals held by the Massachusetts State Archives, Boston.

150 "Clark-McCarthy," *Springfield* (MA) *Republican*, 28 October 1897, p. 10, col. 3; digital image, *GenealogyBank* (http://www.genealogybank.com : accessed 6 Jul 2013).

151 Ibid.

152 Registry of Vital Records and Statistics, "Massachusetts, Births, 1841-1915," index and images, *FamilySearch* (http://www.familysearch.org : accessed 7 Oct 2013, vol. 485, p. 250, no. 1411, John Patrick McCarthy; FHL microfilm 1,843,711; originals held by the Massachusetts State Archives, Boston.

153 Massachusetts Registry of Vital Records and Statistics, "Massachusetts, Births, 1841-1915," index and images, *FamilySearch* (http://www.familysearch.org : accessed 8 Aug 2013); 1902, p. 251, no. 9, Anna McCarthy; FHL microfilm 2,057,388; originals held by the Massachusetts State Archives, Boston.

154 Registry of Vital Records and Statistics, "Massachusetts, Births, 1841-1915," index and images, *FamilySearch* (http://www.familysearch.org : accessed 8 Aug 2013); 1905, p. 262, no. 158, Timothy J. McCarthy; FHL microfilm 2,057,531; originals held by the Massachusetts State Archives, Boston.

155 "Massachusetts, Births, 1841-1915," database, *FamilySearch* (http://www.familysearch.org : accessed 8 Aug 2013), entry for Katherine McCarthy, born 6 May 1908 in Northampton, Hampshire County, Massachusetts; FHL microfilm 2,315,250.

156 Hampshire County, Massachusetts, Johanna McCarthy probate file 13287, Hampshire County Probate and Family Court; Northampton.

157 Ibid.

158 Ibid.

159 Hampshire County, Massachusetts, "Unindexed Property," Book 551: 9, Patrick McCarthy, Plan of Lots, July 1901, digital image, Secretary of the Commonwealth-Registry of Deeds, Hampshire District Registry of Deeds (http://www.sec.state.ma.us/rod/rodhamp/hampidx.htm : accessed 8 May 2014.

160 Massachusetts Registry of Vital Records and Statistics, "Massachusetts Deaths, 1841-1915," index and images, *FamilySearch* (http://www.familysearch.org : accessed 22 Aug 2011), 1901, n.p., no. 7, William Conners; FHL microfilm 2,057,733; originals held by the Massachusetts State Archives, Boston. William died of tuberculosis.

161 Hampshire County, Massachusetts, death certificate unnumbered (1902), John Clark, City Clerk's Office, Northampton.

162 "Northampton," *Daily Hampshire Gazette*, 10 Feb 1902, n.p., col. 4; (Northampton, Mass.: H.S Gere and Sons 1890-); "*Daily Hampshire Gazette* [microform]," Dec. 19, 1901-Mar. 31, 1902; microfilm held by Forbes Library, Northampton, MA.

163 Hampshire Co., MA, death certificate unnumbered (1902), John Clark.

164 "Massachusetts Death Records, 1841-1915," *Ancestry.com*, database and images, death certificate, p. 59, (reg.) no. 100 (1907), Patrick McCarthy Jr.. Patrick was a student, apparently in Nova Scotia, Canada at the time of his death.

165 "Massachusetts Deaths, 1841-1915," *FamilySearch*, database and images, 1907, p. 207, no. 248, Catherine (McCarthy) Bishop. Catherine died of pulmonary tuberculosis.

166 "THE CAUCUS PROBABILITIES," *Springfield* (MA) *Republican*, 13 November 1907, p. 9, col. 1, digital image, *GenealogyBank* (http://www.genealogybank.com : accessed 9 June 2014.

167 "Field Day of the Labor Unions," *Springfield* (MA) *Republican*, 2 Sept 1902, p. 5, no col.; digital image, *GenealogyBank* (http://www.genealogybank.com : accessed 20 Apr 2010).

168 "Field Day of the Labor Unions," *Springfield* (MA) *Republican*, 2 Sept 1902, p. 5, no col.

169 "The Field Day at Northampton, Weather a Disappointment," *Springfield* (MA) *Republican*, 14 Sept 1902, p. 5, col. 4; digital image, *GenealogyBank* (http://www.genealogybank.com : accessed 30 Aug 2013).

170 Hampshire County, Massachusetts, death certificate no. 91 (1904), Joseph Clark; City Clerk's Office, Northampton. The certificate noted that it was a difficult birth.

171 "Capital and Labor at Bay State the Northampton Cutleries," *Springfield* (MA) *Republican*, 29 Dec 1907, p. 16, no col.; digital image, *GenealogyBank* (http://www.genealogybank.com : accessed 14 July 2014.)

172 "Hampshire County: Northampton," *Springfield* (MA) *Republican*, 21 Sept 1905, p. 9, col. 2; digital image, *GenealogyBank* (http://www.genealogybank.com : accessed 25 July 2013).

173 Clark, The Clark Chronicles, n.p.

174 1910 U.S. census, Hampshire County, Massachusetts, population schedule, Northampton, Enumeration District (ED) 705, sheet 4-A (penned) -sheet 5-B (penned), dwelling 71-105, families 75-110, Mildred McNamara-Edward J. Jarvis; database and images, *Ancestry.com* (http://www.ancestry.com : accessed 22 Sept 2013); citing FHL microfilm 1,374,606; National Archives microfilm publication T624_593.

175 1910 U.S. census, Hampshire County, Massachusetts, population schedule, Northampton, (ED) 705, p. 150 (stamped), sheet 4-A (penned), dwelling 77, family 81, Edward Sanier; database and images, *Ancestry.com* (http://www.ancestry.com : accessed 22 Sept 2013); citing National Archives microfilm publication T624_593; FHL microfilm 1,374,606. Edward was enumerated as a thirteen-year-old cutlery inspector. The entry for his seventeen-year-old sister states that she attended school since 1 September 1909.

176 1910 U.S. census, Hampshire County, Massachusetts, population schedule, Northampton, Enumeration District (ED) 705, p. 150 (stamped), sheet 4-A (penned), dwelling 73, family 77, Leo Clark; digital image, *Ancestry.com* (http://www.ancestry.com : accessed 8 Sept 2013); citing National Archives microfilm publication T624_59; FHL microfilm 1,374,606.

177 Ibid.

178 *Wikipedia* (http://www.wikipedia.org : accessed 6 Mar 2014), "Penal Laws (Ireland)," rev.23:38, 14 February 2014.

179 Clark, "The Clark Chronicles," 4.

180 *Wikipedia* (http://www.wikipedia.org), "Scarlet fever," rev. 02:51, 24 Sept 2013.

181 Physician and Surgeons of the Principal London Hospitals, *The Family Physician: A Manual of Domestic Medicine* (London, Paris, New York and

Melborne: Cassell & Company, Limited, 1886), p. 45; digital images, *Google Books* (http://www.googlebooks.com/books : accessed 27 Sept 2013).

182 Mae related this story to the author when she was a young girl.

183 Northampton, Massachusetts, death certificate no.138 (1915), Cornelius Cashman, City Clerk's Office, Northampton.

184 "Death of Cornelius Cashman," *Daily Hampshire (MA) Gazette*, 15 April 1915, p. 3, col. 10; (Northampton, Mass.: H.S Gere and Sons 1890-); "*Daily Hampshire Gazette* [microform], Feb. 27, 1915-May 14, 1915; microfilm held by Forbes Library, Northampton, MA.

185 *Northampton City Directory, 1915*: (Northampton, MA: The Price and Lee Co., 1915), 109, entry for "Cleary, Wilber" [Cleary, Wilbur]; digital image, *Ancestry.com* (http://www.ancestry.com : 1 Oct 2013).

186 "New Hampshire Birth Records, Early to 1900," database, *FamilySearch* (http://www.familysearch.org : accessed 16 April 2012), index entry for "Wilber Edward Clary [Wilbur Edward Cleary]," born 27 Oct. 1893 in Bennington, Hillsborough, County; FHL microfilm 1,000,375.

187 Hillsborough County, New Hampshire, death certificate no. 51 (1937), Andrew M. Cleary, Town Clerk's Office, Bennington. "New Hampshire Deaths and Burials," database, *FamilySearch.org* (http://www.familysearch.org : accessed 28 Feb 2011), entry for Margaret C. Cleary died 9 Sept. 1924 in Bennington, Hillsborough County, New Hampshire; FHL microfilm 2,168,696.

188 Personal knowledge of Gladys Newhall, Oral interview, 17 Nov 1984. Gladys, the daughter of Eileen (Cleary) Newhall, stated that "Maggie" was not a well woman. Gladys was a witness to one of her seizures during a family outing.

189 1900 U.S. census, Norfolk County, Virginia, population schedule, Tanner's Creek, Enumeration District (ED) 38, p. 135-A (stamped), sheet 49 (penned), dwelling 807, family 917; Wilber Cleary [Wilbur Cleary]; digital images, *Ancestry.com* (http://www.ancestry.com : accessed 1 Oct 2013); citing National Archives microfilm publication T623; FHL microfilm publication 1,241,719.

190 1910 U.S. census, Norfolk County, Virginia, population schedule, Norfolk, Enumeration District (ED) 22, sheet 5-A (penned), p. 50 (stamped), dwelling 51, family 64; Wilber Cleary [Wilbur Cleary]; digital images, *Ancestry.com* (http://www.ancestry.com : accessed 1 Oct 2013); citing National Archives microfilm publication T624_1637. Wilbur was employed in a cutlery.

191 Margaret (Cleary) Leitl, daughter of Wilbur Cleary [ADDRESS FOR PRIVATE USE,] Easthampton, Massachusetts, interview by Elizabeth Banas, 19 March 1999, notes held by interviewer, [ADDRESS FOR PRIVATE USE,] Belchertown, Massachusetts. Anne (Cleary) Goodhind, daughter of Wilbur Cleary [ADDRESS FOR PRIVATE USE,] Palmer, Massachusetts, interview by Elizabeth Banas, 19 March 1999, notes held by interviewer, [ADDRESS FOR PRIVATE USE,] Belchertown, Massachusetts. This interview with Anne and Peg occurred in the Red Rock restaurant in Easthampton.

192 Personal knowledge of Gladys Newhall, Oral interview, 17 Nov 1984.

193 Elizabeth Banas, *Mary's Garden*, n.p.

194 1900 U.S. census, Hillsborough County, New Hampshire, population schedule, Bennington, Enumeration District (ED) 79, sheet 1-B (penned), dwelling 17, family 20, Ferdinand Dobler; digital image, *Ancestry.com* (http://www.ancestry.com : accessed 8 December 2013); citing National Archives microfilm publication T623; FHL microfilm 1,240,947. Ferdinand was enumerated as a "cutler grinder."

195 Registry of Vital Records and Statistics, "Massachusetts State Vital Records, 1841-1920," database and images, *FamilySearch* (http://www.familysearch. org : accessed 20 April 2015), vol. 644, p. 349, no. 49, Wilbur E. Cleary and Mary H. Clark; originals held by the Massachusetts State Archives, Boston.

196 "Clark-Cleary," *Daily Hampshire* (MA) *Gazette*, 18 Apr 1917, p. 3 col., 1; (Northampton, Mass.: H.S Gere and Sons 1890-), n.p.; "*Daily Hampshire Gazette* [microform]," Feb. 20,1917-May 10, 1917; microfilm held by Forbes Library, Northampton, MA.

197 Birth, death and marriage data have been withheld by the author.

198 Ibid.

199 Social Security Administration, "U.S. Social Security Death Index," database, Genealogybank.com (http://www.genealogybank.com : accessed 15 Aug 2012), entry for Wilbur E. Cleary, 1964, S.S. no. redacted.

200 Social Security Administration, "U.S. Social Security Death Index," database, Genealogybank.com (http://www.genealogybank.com : accessed 15 Aug 2012), entry for Mary H. Cleary, S.S. no. redacted.

201 "United States Public Records Index, database, *FamilySearch* (http://www. familysearch.org : accessed 18 Dec 2013), index entry for "Margaret M. Leitl," born 28 Feb 1918; citing FHL record no. 4206482.

202 *Wikipedia* (http://www.wikipedia.org), "Selective Service Act of 1917," rev. 19:05, 12 November 2013.

203 *Wikipedia*, (http://www.wikipedia.org), "Archduke Franz Ferdinand of Austria," rev. 16:12, 4 December 2013.

204 *Wikipedia*, "Selective Service Act of 1917," rev. 03:18, 16 Sept 2013. Archduke Franz Ferdinand was the Austro- Hungarian prince of Hungary and Bohemia.

205 "World War I Draft Registration Cards, 1917-1918," digital images, *Ancestry.com* (http://www.ancestry.com accessed 3 Feb 2011), card for Leo Ernest Clark, no. 12, Northampton Draft Board 5; citing *World War I Selective Service System Draft Registration Cards, 1917-1918,* National Archives microfilm publication M1509, imaged from FHL microfilm 1,684,479.

206 "World War I Draft Registration Cards, 1917-1918," digital images, *Ancestry.com*, card for Leo Ernest Clark, no. 12, Northampton Draft Board 5

207 *Northampton and Easthampton Directory* (Northampton, MA: The Price, Lee and Co, 1917), 107, entries for "Clark, Leo and James"; digital image, *Ancestry.com* (http://www.ancestry.com : accessed 8 Oct 2013). "World War I Draft Registration Cards, 1917-1918," digital images, *Ancestry.com*, card for Leo Ernest Clark, no. 12, Northampton Draft Board 5. Leo was living at home with his parents. The address entered on the card was the family residence.

208 Ibid.

209 "World War I Draft Registration Cards, 1917-1918," digital image, *Ancestry.com*, card for Raymond Clark Beckett, no. 3, Providence Draft Board 3; citing *World War I Selective Service System Draft Registration Cards, 1917-1918,* National Archives microfilm publication M1509, imaged from FHL microfilm 1,852,402. "World War I Draft Registration Cards, 1917-1918," digital images, *Ancestry.com*, card for Edward John Beckett, no. 206, Providence Draft Board 3; citing *World War I Selective Service System Draft Registration Cards, 1917-1918,* National Archives microfilm publication M1509, imaged from FHL microfilm 1,852,402.

210 "World War I Draft Registration Cards, 1917-1918," digital images, *Ancestry.com*, card for Raymond Clark Beckett, no. 3, Providence Draft Board 3.

211 "World War I Draft Registration Cards, 1917-1918," digital images, *Ancestry.com*, card for Edward John Beckett, no. 206, Providence Draft Board 3. "Rhode Island, Marriages, 1851-1920," database, *Ancestry.com* (http://www.ancestry.com : accessed 23 Oct 2013), entry for Edward J. Beckett and Elizabeth McElroy, 25 Apr 1917, Rhode Island.

212 "World War I Draft Registration Cards, 1917-1918," digital images, *Ancestry.com*, card for Edward J. Beckett, no. 206, Providence Draft Board 3.

213 "World War I Draft Registration Cards, 1917-1918," database and digital images, *Ancestry.com*, card for Edward John Beckett, no. 206, Providence Draft Board 3. "World War I Draft Registration Cards, 1917-1918, database and digital images, *Ancestry.com*, card for Raymond Clark Beckett, no. 3, Providence Draft Board 3. Edward was employed as an electrician for the NY, NH & H Railroad. Raymond was employed as rail— for the same company.

214 "World War I Draft Registration Cards, 1917-1918," database and digital images, *Ancestry.com* (http://www.ancestry.com : accessed 3 Mar 2014), card for John P. McCarthy, no. —, Northampton Draft Board 5; citing *World War I Selective Service Draft Registration Cards 1917-1918*, National Archives Microfilm Publication M1509, imaged from FHL microfilm 1,684,518.

215 Ibid.

216 Ibid.

217 John P. McCarthy (5527005) entry, roster of Northampton, Massachusetts veterans who served in World War I; Adjutant Generals Office, Archives-Museum Branch, Concord, Massachusetts

218 Ibid.

219 Ibid.

220 Ibid.

221 "To Go to Camp Upton Monday," *Springfield (MA) Republican*, 22 May 1918, p. 15, col. 6; digital image, *GenealogyBank* (http://www.genealogy-bank.com : accessed 10 July 2013). This news article reported the names of 26 men drafted to meet the quota.

222 Leo Ernest Clark (3,192,595, Pvt.) World War I military data card, undated; Adjutant Generals Office, Archives-Museum Branch, Massachusetts.

223 *Wikipedia* (http://www.wikipedia.com), "Battle of Vittorio Veneto," rev. 06:48, 4 December 2013.

224 Leo Ernest Clark (Pvt.), Form no. 724-1, A.G.O., 15 June 1921, no. 3777, Records of the Adjutant General's Office.

225 Ibid.

226 The author's mother (Anne (Cleary) Goodhind) told her this story.

227 "New Hampshire Births and Christenings, 1714-1904," database, *FamilySearch* (http://www.familysearch.org : accessed 20 Dec 2013), entry for Walter Gottlieb Dobbler [Dobler] born 22 March 1898, Bennington, Hillsborough; FHL microfilm 2,168,696.

228 *Northampton and Easthampton Directory* (Northampton: The Price, Lee and Co., 1902), 55, "Dobler, Ferdinand"; also subsequent years by the same title: (1910) 108, (1916) 125, entry for "Dobler, Frederick [Ferdinand]"; digital image, *Ancestry.com* (http://www.ancestry.com : accessed 17 Oct 2013).

229 1900 U.S. census, Hillsboro [Hillsborough] Co., N.H., pop. sch., Bennington, (ED) 79, sheet 1-B, dwell. 17, fam. 20, Ferdinand Dobler household.

230 Hampshire County, Massachusetts, Marriages, Book 4:66 for Walter Dobler-Helen Clark, 1920; City Clerk's Office, Northampton. The marriage was performed by Father Broderick, pastor of Blessed Sacrament Church.

231 1920 U.S. census, Hampshire County, Massachusetts, population schedule, Northampton, Enumeration District (ED) 173, sheet 1-B, dwelling 13, family 15, Helen C. Clark; digital image, *Ancestry.com* (http://www.ancestry,com : accessed 17 Oct 2013); National Archives microfilm publication T625_705.

232 "1920 United States Census," database, *Ancestry.com* (http://www.ancestry.com : accessed 15 Oct 2013), Massachusetts, entry for Walter Dobbel [Dobler], 21, City of Springfield, Hampden County.

233 Ibid.

234 *Northampton, Massachusetts, City Directory*, 1920 (Northampton, MA : The Price, Lee and Co., 1920), 111, entry for Dobler, Mrs. Walter"; digital image, *Ancestry.com* (http://www.ancestry.com : accessed 18 Oct 2013).

235 *Springfield, Massachusetts City Directory* (The Price, Lee and Co., 1924), 372, entry for "Dobler, Walter"; digital image, *Ancestry.com* (http://www.ancestry.com : accessed 18 Oct 2013); also subsequent years by the same title: (1925) 373, (1926) 357, (1927) 363.

236 *The Greater Hartford Directory* (Hartford, Connecticut: The Price, Lee and Co., 1931), 786, "Dobler, Walter"; digital image, *Ancestry.com* (http://www. ancestry.com : accessed 18 Oct 2013); also subsequent years by the same title: (1940) 661, (1951-1952) 784; Walter's entry states that he was a polisher and later a foreman.

237 *The Greater Hartford Directory* (Hartford, Connecticut: The Price, Lee and Co., 1931), 786, "Dobler, Walter"; digital image, *Ancestry.com* (http://www. ancestry.com : accessed 19 Oct 2013); also subsequent years by the same title: (1940) 661, (1951-1952) 784.

238 Birth, death and marriage data have been withheld by the author.

239 Social Security Administration, "U.S. Social Security Death Index," database, *GenealogyBank.com* (http://www.genealogybank.com : accessed 15 Aug 2012), entry for Helen Catherine Clark, 1979, S.S. no. redacted.

240 Connecticut Department of Health, "Connecticut Death Index, 1949-2001," database, *Ancestry.com* (http://ancestry.com : accessed 27 Sept. 2013), entry for Walter Paul Dobler, died 5 Nov 1981, Newington, Hartford County.

241 U.S. Social Security Administraton, "Social Security Death Index," database, *Ancestry.com* (http://www.ancestry.com : accessed 24 Dec 2013), entry for Roger J. Cleary, no. 019-16-0624.

242 Hampshire County, Massachusetts, unindexed property, Clement Manufacturing to James Clark, mortgage, Book 757: 17, 26 April 1920; digital image, Massachusetts Secretary of State, *Registry of Deeds*(http://www. masslandrecords.com : accessed 18 Oct 2013).

243 Hampshire County, Massachusetts, unindexed property, James Clark to Mary Clark, deed, Book 756: 459, 26 April 1920; digital image, Massachusetts Secretary of State, *Registry of Deeds* (http://www.masslandrecords.com accessed 18 Oct 2013,

244 Elizabeth Banas, *Mary's Garden*, n.p.

245 Margaret (Cleary) Leitl, interview, 19 Mar 1999.

246 Ibid.

247 Ibid.

248 Ibid.

249 Ibid.

250 Ibid.

251 Ibid.

252 Hampshire County, Massachusetts, Deaths, Vol. 4 (1922): 221, Thomas Conners; City Clerk's office, Northampton.

253 "Massachusetts, Births, 1841-1915," database, *FamilySearch* (http://www. familysearch.org : accessed 12 Dec 2012), entry for James F. Connors, born 4 Feb 1904, Northampton, Hampshire County, Massachusetts; FHL microfilm 2,057,437.

254 Margaret Donaghey, New Hampshire [EMAIL ADDRESS FOR PRIVATE USE], to Elizabeth Banas, email, 23 Oct 2013, "Question," James Clark Family, Leo Clark, research files; privately held by Elizabeth Banas, [(E-ADDRESS & STREET ADDRESS FOR PRIVATE USE,] Belchertown, Massachusetts.

255 Registry of Vital Records and Statistics, "Massachusetts Deaths 1841-1915," index and images, *FamilySearch* (http://www.familyse-arch.org : accessed 9 March 2014), 1911, p. 195, no. 198, Annie (Droney) Casey; FHL microfilm 2,396,048; originals held by the Massachusetts State Archives, Boston. The cause of death was pneumonia.

256 Registry of Vital Records and Statistics, "Massachusetts Deaths, 1841-1915," index and images, *FamilySearch* (http://www.familysearch.com : accessed 9 March 2014), 1911, p. 330, no. 243, Ellen Whalen; FHL microfilm 2,396,048; originals held by the Massachusetts State Archives, Boston. Cause of death was gastro-enteritis and senility (secondary).

257 Margaret Donaghey, Claremont, New Hampshire [(E-ADDRESS FOR PRIVATE USE),] to Elizabeth Banas, e-mail, 3 Jan 2014, "RE:," James Clark Family, Leo Clark, research files; privately held by Elizabeth Banas, [(E-ADDRESS), & STREET ADDRESS FOR PRIVATE USE], Belchertown, Massachusetts.

258 Donaghey to Banas, e-mail, 23 Oct 2013.

259 Hampshire County, Massachusetts, Marriages, 4: 144, for Clark-Casey, City Clerk's Office, Northampton.

260 Hampshire County, Massachusetts, probate case file, Box 453: 26, Lizzie Casey (1928), Account of Debt, 8 February 1928; Probate Clerk's Office, Northampton.

261 Hampshire County, Massachusetts, Deeds, Book 844: 225, Estate of Lizzie Casey to Margaret Clark, 6 March 1928; Hampshire County Registry of Deeds, Northampton.

262 Hampshire Co., MA, Deeds, Book 844:225. The sale price noted on the deed was $2800.

263 Birth, death and marriage data have been withheld by the author

264 Hampshire County, Massachusetts, death certificate (1968), Leo E. Clark; City Clerk's Office, Northampton.

265 U.S. Social Security Administration, "Social Security Death Index," database, Ancestry.com (http://www.ancestry.com : accessed 24 Feb 2014), entry for Margaret M. Clark, no. 021-30-9367.

266 "Death of Mrs. Bridget Cashman," Daily Hampshire (MA) Gazette, 21 Nov 1924, p. 11, col., 5; (Northampton, Mass.: H.S Gere and Sons 1890----), n.p.; "Daily Hampshire Gazette [microform]," November 1924-December 1924; microfilm held by Forbes Library, Northampton, MA. Courtesy of the Daily Hampshire Gazette.

267 Rathcormac District, Ireland, Marriage Records, 1865, Cashman-McGrath; General Register Office, Dublin. A certified birth record was unavailable. The year of birth was calculated by the age noted on the certified copy of the marriage register entry.

268 Connecticut Department of State Vital Records, death certificate unnumbered (1925), Ellen Catherine Holleran; Department of Public Health, Hartford.

269 "Rhode Island, Marriages, 1851-1920," database, *Ancestry.com* (http://www.ancestry.com : accessed 23 Oct 2013), entry for Edward J. Beckett and Elizabeth McElroy, 25 Apr 1917, Rhode Island.

270 1930 U.S. Federal census, Providence County, Rhode Island, population schedule, Providence, Enumeration District (ED) 4-123, sheet 3-A(penned), p. 219 (stamped), dwelling 22, family 50, Florence Selwyn; digital image, *Ancestry.com* (http://www. Ancestry. com : accessed 23 Oct 2013); National Archives microfilm publication T626_2183. The date of marriage was calculated via Florence's entry for "Age at first marriage" (20 years old). Florence is entered as the wife of William Selwyn.

271 John Ennis, compiler, Descendants of Hugh Clark, report to Elizabeth A. Banas, [ADDRESS FOR PRIVATE USE,] Belchertown, Massachusetts,

n.d., photocopy held by [Elizabeth Banas, Belchertown, Massachusetts]. Report notes that Anna (Annie) married James A. Ennis (1916).

272 1925 Rhode Island State census, Providence County, population schedule, Providence, Enumeration Distirct (ED) 218, pp. 10-11 (penned), dwelling 43, family 78, Mary (Mae) Beckett, digital image, *FamilySearch* (http://www.familysearch.org : accessed 11 May 2015); FHL microfilm 1,769,421.

273 Ibid. Ruth H. Beckett.

274 Ibid. Raymond Beckett.

275 "Massachusetts Marriage Index, 1901-1955 and 1966-1970," database and index, Ancestry.*com* (http://www.ancestry.com : accessed 25 Oct 2013), entry for John Patrick McCarthy, Vol. 92; citing the Registry of Vital Records and Statistics, Vol. 42, p. 479; Massachusetts State Archives, Boston.

276 "Massachusetts Births, 1841-1915," *FamilySearch*, database and images, 1902, p. 251, no.7, Anna McCarthy.

277 "Massachusetts, Births, 1841-1915," *FamilySearch*, database and images, 1905, p. 262. no. 158, Timothy J. McCarthy.

278 "Massachusetts Births, 1841-1915," *FamilySearch*, database, 6 May 1908, Catherine Marie McCarthy.

279 "Massachusetts, Births, 1841-1915," *FamilySearch*, database and images, 1902, p. 252, no. 73, John George Clark.

280 "Massachusetts Births, 1841-1915," *FamilySearch* database and images, 1905, p. 268, no. 444, William Cornelius Clark.

281 Providence County, Rhode Island, death certificate 83 (1925), Mary Hannah Beckett, Rhode Island State Archives, Providence. Other contributing causes of death were atherosclerosis, myocarditis and nephritis.

282 John Ennis, interview, 6 September 2013.

283 "New York, New York, Marriage Indexes. 1866-1937," database, Ancestry. com (http://www.ancestry.com : accessed 10 Apr 2014), index entry for Bertha C. Anderson, married Raymond C. Beckett, 21 January 1932, New York City, New York.

284 David McElroy, Ohio, ([E-ADDRESS FOR PRIVATE USE,] to Elizabeth Banas, e-mail, 18 June 2008, "RE: Looking for more information about Edward John Beckett," John Clark Family, Mary Hannah (Clark) Beckett, Research Files; privately held by Elizabeth Banas, [(E-ADDRESS) & STREET ADDRESS FOR PRIVATE USE,] Belchertown, Massachusetts. David McElroy is Elizabeth (Besse) (McElroy) Beckett's nephew.

285 U.S. Social Security Admnistration, "Social Security Death Index," database, Ancestry.com (http://www.ancestry.com : accessed 23 Oct 2013), entry for Anna Ennis, no. 037-24-5526.

286 U.S. Social Security Administration, "Social Security Death Index," database, Ancestry.com (http://www.ancestry.com : accessed 23 Oct 2013), entry for Raymond Beckett, no. 038-05-4908.

287 U.S. Social Security Administration, "Social Security Death Index," database, Ancestry.com (http://www.ancestry. com : accessed 23 Oct 2013), entry for Florence A. Beckett, no. 038-14-9434.

288 U.S. Social Security Administration, "Social Security Death Index," database, GenealogyBank (http://www.genealogybank.com : accessed 22 Oct 2013), entry for Mary Beckett, no. redacted

289 John Ennis, compiler, Descendants of Hugh Clark, report to Elizabeth A. Banas, [ADDRESS FOR PRIVATE USE,] Belchertown, Massachusetts, n.d., photocopy held by [Elizabeth Banas, Belchertown, Massachusetts]. U.S. Social Security Administration, "Social Security Death Index," database, *GenealogyBank* (http://www.genealogybank.com : accessed 2 May 2014), entry for Ruth H. Morrissey, no. redacted.

290 No death data was located for Edward Beckett.

291 "Rhode Island Deaths and Burials, 1802-1950," database, *FamilySearch* (http://www.familysearch.org : accessed 10 Mar 2014), entry for Edward J. Beckett, died 28 April 1946, Providence, Providence County, Rhode Island; FHL microfilm 2,168,075. Edward's birth date is erroneously entered in this index as 1873.

292 Margaret (Cleary) Leitl, interview, 19 Mar 1999.

293 Connecticut Department of State Vital Records, death certificate, no. 25 (1907), James W. Wheeler; Department of Health, Hartford. The cause of death was "acute dilation of the heart and gastritis simplex."

294 Monroe County, New York, death certificate no. 1247 (1922), John J. Miller, Office of Vital Records, Rochester. The cause of death was lobar pneumonia and pleurisy."

295 "John J. Miller Dead," (Rochester) *Democrat* & *Chronicle*, 18 April 1922, p. 21, col. 2. The obituary noted he owned the Kenmore Hotel and was affiliated with the Traders National Bank.

296 Cathleen (Clark) Smith, interview, October 2013.

297 Margaret (Cleary) Leitl, interview, 19 Mar 1999.

298 Ibid.

299 Cathleen (Clark) Smith, interview, October 2013.

300 John P. Clark, "Growing Up In The Great Depression," n.p., MS, n.d., Fitchburg, Massachusetts; box 1: 83; John G. Clark Collection, Special Collections and University Archives, W.E.B. Du Bois Library, University of Massachusetts, Amherst.

301 "Massachusetts, Births, 1841-1915," database, *FamilySearch* (http://www.familysearch.org : accessed 1 Jan 1024), entry for Ruth Helena Miller, born 8 January 1902, Easthampton, Hampshire County, Massachusetts; FHL microfilm 2,057,388.

302 1880 U.S. census, Hampshire County, Massachusetts, population schedule, Easthampton, Enumeration District (ED) 344, sheet 329-C (stamped), p. 21 (penned), dwelling 122, family 165, Minnie Hupher; digital image, *Ancestry.com* (http://www.ancestry.com : accessed 20 Feb 2014); National Archives microfilm publication T9_537. 1880 U.S. census, Hampshire County, Massachusetts, population schedule, Easthampton, Enumeration District (ED) 344, sheet 329-C (stamped), p. 21 (penned), dwelling 121, family 164, Frank Miller; digital image, *Ancestry.com* (http://www.ancestry.com : accessed 20 Feb 2014); National Archives microfilm publication T9_537. It is unclear whether his father owned the tailoring shop.

303 1910 U.S. census, Hampshire County, Massachusetts, population schedule, Easthampton, Enumeration District (ED) 683, sheet 11-B(penned), dwelling 176, family 273, Frank F. Miller; digital image, *Ancestry.com* (http://www.ancestry.com : accessed 1 January 2014); citing National Archives microfilm publication T624_593; FHL microfilm 1,374,606. Frank Miller's entry notes that he was a tailor and owned a tailoring shop.

304 1880 U.S. census, Hampshire Co., MA,, pop. sch., Easthampton, ED 344, sheet 329-C (stamped), dwell. 122, fam. 165, Minnie Hupher; 1880 U.S. census, Hampshire Co., MA, pop. sch., Easthampton, ED 344, sheet 329-C (stamped), dwell. 121, fam. 164, Frank Miller.

305 Clark, "Growing Up In The Great Depression," n.p.

306 Andrienne (Goggin) Clark, Fitchburg, Massachusetts, to Elizabeth Banas, 18 January 2014, remarks pertaining to the Clark-Miller marriage were recorded by Andrienne Clark in her editorial comments regarding this book; editorial notes and commentary, privately held by Elizabeth Banas, [ADDRESS FOR PRIVATE USE,] Belchertown, Massachusetts. Andrienne recalled that a cousin told her there was tension in the Clark family due to John marrying a Congregationalist.

307 *Wikipedia* (http://www.wikipedia.com : accessed 22 Feb 2014), "Marriage (Catholic Church)," rev. 15:16, 19 February 2014.

308 Banas, *Mary's Garden*, n.p. This fact was not cited.

309 Ibid.

310 Clark to Banas, 18 January 2014. Quotations were taken from Andrienne Clark's editorial notes pertaining to this manuscript.

311 Janet Richer ([ADDRESS FOR PRIVATE USE], Colorado), interview by Elizabeth Banas, 8 March 2014; notes, privately held by Elizabeth Banas, [ADDRESS FOR PRIVATE USE,] Belchertown, Massachusetts. Janet Richer is the niece of Ruth (Miller) Clark.

312 Andrienne (Goggin) Clark, Fitchburg, Massachusetts [(E-ADDRESS FOR PRIVATE USE),] to Elizabeth Banas, e-mail, 18 February 2014, "Oh yes," James Clark Family File, John G. Clark, research files; privately held by

Elizabeth Banas, [(E-ADDRESS) & STREET ADDRESS FOR PRIVATE USE,] Belchertown, Massachusetts.

313 Ibid.

314 Clark, "Growing Up In The Great Depression," n.p.

315 Ibid.

316 Banas, *Mary's Garden*, n.p. This story came to me via Joseph Gilboy, Julia's grandson.

317 1930 U.S. census, Hampshire County, Massachusetts, population schedule, Easthampton, Enumeration District (ED) 8-10, p. 165 (stamped), sheet 19-A (penned), no dwell., family 232, John B. [G.] Clark; digital image, *Ancestry.com* (http://www.ancestry.com : accessed 12 May 2015); FHL microfilm 2,340,647. John G. Clark was erroneously enumerated as John "B" in this census taking. Other, household members enumerated were Minnie, 70, (head) and Ruth M., 28, (daughter). *Northampton, Easthampton Directory* (Springfield, Massachusetts: The Price, Lee & Co., 1928), 108, "Clark, John"; digital image, *Ancestry.com* (http://www.ancestry.com : accessed 12 Mar 2014); also subsequent years by the same title: (1929) 39, (1930) 39, (1931) 38. John's entry notes that his occupation was insurance agent or salesman.

318 Clark, "Growing Up In The Great Depression," n.p.

319 Worcester County, Massachusetts, death certificate no. 171 (1988), John P. Clark, City Clerk's Office, Fitchburg.

320 Andrienne (Goggin) Clark, Fitchburg, Massachusetts [(E-ADDRESS FOR PRIVATE USE),] to Elizabeth Banas, e-mail, 18 April 2014, "Letters," JamesClark Family File, John G. Clark, research files; privately held by Elizabeth Banas, [(E-ADDRESS & STREET ADDRESS FOR PRIVATE

USE,] Belchertown, Massachusetts. "Maud" was John's aunt and Mary Ann's sister.

321 "Massachusetts Births,1841-1915," database, *Ancestry.com* (http://www.ancestry.com : accessed 29 Oct 2013), entry for William Cornelius Clark born 22 Dec 1905, Northampton, Hampshire County.

322 Franklin Co., MA, birth certificate, no.45 (1868), James Clark.

323 Banas, *Mary's Garden*, n.p.

324 Cooley Dickinson Hospital to the Estate of James Clark, invoice, 1 Oct 1927, original, family copy, James Clark Family file, James Clark, privately held by Elizabeth Banas [ADDRESS FOR PRIVATE USE,] Belchertown, Massachusetts, 2004. This invoice was found among the possessions of Mary (Mae) Cleary upon her death (1993) and was presented to Elizabeth Banas by Anne M. Goodhind (Mae's daughter). This invoice noted the date Jimmy was admitted to the hospital.

325 Hampshire County, Massachusetts, death certificate unnumbered (1927), James M. Clark, City Clerk's Office, Northampton. Jimmy died on 22 August 1927.

326 "Obituary," *Daily Hampshire (MA) Gazette*, 23 Aug 1927, p. 3, col. 3. Courtesy of the Daily Hampshire Gazette.

327 Margaret (Cleary) Leitl, interview, 19 Mar 1999.

328 St. Mary's Cemetery Office (Northampton, Massachusetts), card file. The location of the lot is noted as Lot 7, Range 3. Card file noted the internment date.

329 "Here and There with T.F.F.," John G. Clark Family Papers. Courtesy of the *Daily Hampshire Gazette*.

330 Hampshire County, Massachusetts, no. 100 (1927), Frank F. Miller; City Clerk's office, Easthampton.

331 Clark, "The Clark Chronicles," 10.

332 "Calls for Fire Department," *Springfield* (MA) *Republican*, 26 December 1928, p. 13, col. 6; digital image, *GenealogyBank* (http://www.genealogy-bank.com : accessed 4 April 2014). Courtesy of the *Springfield Republican*.

333 Ibid.

334 1930 U.S. census, Hampshire County, Massachusetts, population schedule, Northampton, Enumeration District (ED) 8-35, sheet 2-B(penned), dwelling 16, family 23, Thomas Wade, digital image, *Ancestry.com* (http://www.ancestry.com : accessed 4 April 2014); FHL microfilm 2,340,647.

335 Connecticut Department of Health, "Connecticut Death Index, 1949-2001," database, *Ancestry.com* (http://www.ancestry.com : accessed 17 Nov 2008), entry for Nathalie (Coffron) Clark, unnumbered (1991).

336 James Bills, E. Hartford, Connecticut [(E-ADDRESS FOR PRIVATE USE),] to Elizabeth Banas, e-mail, 6 March 2009, "Re: Mystery Photos Solved," James Clark Family File, William Clark, research files; privately held by Elizabeth Banas, [(E-ADDRESS) & STREET ADDRESS FOR PRIVATE USE,] Belchertown, MA.

337 Hampshire County, Massachusetts, "Marriages," 4: 262, for Clark-Coffron, City Clerk's Office, Northampton.

338 1930 U.S. census, Hampshire County, Massachusetts, population schedule, Northampton, Enumeration District (ED) 8-34, sheet 15-A (penned), p.181 (stamped), dwelling 306, family 350, William Clark; digital image, *Ancestry.com* (http://www.ancestry.com : accessed 30 Oct 2013); FHL microfilm 2,340,647.

339 *The Greater Hartford Directory, 1945* (Hartford, Connecticut: The Price, Lee & Co., 1945), 726, "Clark, William"; digital image, *Ancestry.com* (http://www.ancestry.com : accessed 3 January 2014); also subsequent years by the same title: (1951-1952) 707, (1955) 716. "Connecticut Death Index, 1949-2001," *Ancestry.com* database entry for William C. Clark, unnumbered (1961). William's address at the time of his death was Hartford, Connecticut.

340 Birth, death and marriage data have been withheld by the author. This information was provided by James Bills.

341 "Connecticut death Index, 1949-2001," database, *Ancestry.com* (http://www.ancestry.com : accessed 17 Nov 2008), index entry for William Cornelius Clark, State File # 06509 (1961), Hartford, Hartford County, Connecticut.

342 "Connecticut death Index, 1949-2001," database, *Ancestry.com* (http://www.ancestry.com : accessed 17 Nov 2008), index entry for Nathalie (Coffron) Clark, State File # 10500 (1991), Hartford, Hartford, County, Connecticut.

343 "Connecticut death Index, 1949-2001," *Ancestry.com* database entry for William Cornelius Clark, State File # 06509 (1961); "Connecticut death Index, 1949-2001," *Ancestry.com* database entry for Nathalie (Coffron) Clark,, State File #10500 (1991).

344 *The Northampton Easthampton Directory*, 1931, (Springfield, Massachusetts: The Price, Lee & Co., 1931), 106, "Clark, William"; digital image, *Ancestry.com* (http://www.ancestry.com : accessed 5 January 2013); also subsequent years by the same title: (1932) 104, (1933) 101, (1934) 94, (1937) 168. The 1937 directory noted that was removed to Hartford (Connecticut).

345 U.S. Department of Labor, "Wages and Hours of Labor," *Monthly Labor Review*, 11 (December 1920); online archives, *JSTOR* (http://www.jstor.org : accessed 3 January 2014).

346 "DaveManuel.com: Inflation Calculator," database, *Davemanuel.com* (http://www.davemanuel.com : accessed 3 January 2014).

347 *Northampton Massachusetts City Directory* (Northampton, Massachusetts: The Price, Lee & Co., 1929), 101, "Clark, William"; digital image, *Ancestry.com* (http://www.ancestry.com : accessed 3 Mar 1014); also subsequent years by the same title: (1930) 102, (1931) 106, (1932) 104.

348 1930 U.S. census, Hampshire Co., MA, pop. sch., Northampton, ED 8-34, sheet 15-A, dwell. 306, fam. 350, William Clark-Mary A. Clark.

349 1930 U.S. census, Hartford County, Connecticut, population schedule, Ward 8 Hartford, Enumeration District (ED) 0052, sheet 23-B (penned), dwelling 206, family 514, Margaret L. Miller; digital image, *Ancestry.com* (http://www.ancestry.com : accessed 18 April 2014); citing National Archives microfilm publication T626_264; FHL microfilm 2,339,999.

350 Hartford County, Connecticut, District of Hartford, Wills & Inventories, 1932: 409, Estate of Margaret L. Miller: Inventory, 1932; Court of Probate, Hartford. The inventory of Maud's estate revealed her possessions, including a bank account and jewelry were valued at $2120.

351 *The Northampton Easthampton Directory*, 1930, (Springfield, Massachusetts: The Price, Lee & Co., 1930), 101, "Clark, Leo"; digital image, *Ancestry.com* (http://www.ancestry.com : accessed 11 Mar 2014); also subsequent years by the same title: (1931) 106, (1932) 103, (1934) 94, (1936) 168, (1937) 167.

352 Cathleen (Clark) Smith, daughter of Leo and Margaret (Casey) Clark ([ADDRESS FOR PRIVATE USE,] Hadley, Massachusetts), interview by Elizabeth Banas, 4 January 2014, notes privately held by interviewer, [ADDRESS FOR PRIVATE USE,] Belchertown, Massachusetts, 2013.

353 Connecticut, death certificate no. 916 (1932), Margaret Miller.

354 Ibid.

355 Margaret Miller Will, 18 January 1932, Hartford, January 1932, p. 276-277; Court of Probate, State of Connecticut, Hartford.

356 Ibid. Julia received one hundred-fifty dollars and Mary Ann received one hundred dollars.

357 Ibid.

358 Ibid.

359 Ibid.

360 Ibid. Margaret was Julia (Cashman) Foran's daughter.

361 Ibid. Edward was married to Helen (Ellen) Cashman (1866-1925). Helen was known as Ellen by the family.

362 Ibid. John G. Clark did not receive a legacy nor was his name mentioned in the will.

363 Hampshire County, Massachusetts, unindexed property, Book 897: 295, Homeowners Loan Corporation to Mary A. Clark, mortgage, 8 August 1934; digital image, Massachusetts Secretary of State, *Registry of Deeds* (http://www.masslandrecords.com : accessed 6 Nov 2013).

364 Hampshire Co., MA, Unindexed Property, Book 757: 17, Clement Manufacturing to Clark, mortgage, Apr. 1920; 11 Feb 1927, James transferred the property to Mary Ann (Book 756: 459).

365 Hampshire County, Massachusetts, unindexed property, Book 930: 450, Homeowners Loan Corporation, Entry to Foreclose Mortgage, 20

December 1937; digital image, Massachusetts Secretary of State, *Registry of Deeds* (http://www.masslandrecords.com : accessed 6 Nov 2013).

366 Hampshire County, Massachusetts, unindexed property, Book 954: 330, Homeowners Loan Corporation to John P. Shea et ux, 7 October 1940; digital image, Massachusetts Secretary of State, *Registry of Deeds* (http://www.masslandrecords.com : accessed 6 Nov 2013).

367 Hampshire County, Massachusetts, "Deaths," Book 7: 24, no. 195, Timothy McCarthy; City Clerk's Office, Northampton.

368 "Last Rites Are Held For Timothy M'Carthy," *Springfield* (MA) *Republican*, 14 May 1935, p. 11, col. 2; digital image, *GenealogyBank* (http://www.genealogbank.com : accessed 16 Feb 2914); Courtesy of the *Springfield Republican*.

369 Ibid.

370 Doyle-McCarthy marriage, notation in Annie (Myers) Egan Scrapbook. Handwritten notation of Marie Doyle and John McCarthy's wedding date, 1924.

371 "McCarthy-Smith," *Springfield (MA) Daily Republican*, 12 September 1928, p. 4, col. 6; digital image, *GenealogyBank* (http:www.genealogybank.com : accessed 16 Feb 2014). Courtesy of the *Springfield Daily Republican*. The marriage occurred 10 September 1928.

372 "Anna Crabbe Marries," *Springfield (MA) Republican*, 20 October 1931, p. 3, col. 6; digital image, *GenealogyBank* (http://www.genealogybank.com : accessed 16 Feb 2014). Courtesy of the *Springfield Republican*. The marriage occurred 19 October 1931.

373 "M'Carthy-Keefe, Church Wedding," *Springfield* (MA) *Republican*, 28 September 1937, p. 12, col.3; digital image, *Ancestry.com* (http://www.ancestry.com : accessed 5 Mar 2014). Courtesy of the *Springfield Republican*.

374 Margaret (Cleary) Leitl, interview, 19 Mar 1999.

375 *Greater Hartford Directory*, 1937 (Hartford, Connecticut: The Price, Lee and Co., 1937), 638, entry for "Clark, William;" digital image, *Ancestry.com* (http://www.ancestry.com : accessed 31 January 2014). William's employment was entered as "polisher."

376 Clark, "Growing Up In The Great Depression," n.p.

377 Ibid.

378 Ibid.

379 Ibid.

380 Ibid.

381 Ibid.

382 Ibid.

383 Ibid.

384 *Wikipedia* (http://www.wikipedia.org : accessed 26 Jan 2014), "Recession of 1937-38," rev. 21:52, 23 Oct 2013.

385 Clark, "Growing Up In The Great Depression," n.p

386 Ibid.

387 *Wikipedia*, "Recession of 1937-38," rev. 21:52, 23 October 2013.

388 Clark, "Growing Up In The Great Depression," n.p.

389 Janet (Royal) Richer ([STREET ADDRESS FOR PRIVATE USE], Colorado Springs, Col.) telephone interview, 8 March 2014; interview by ElizabethBanas, notes held by Banas, [ADDRESS FOR PRIVATE USE,] Belchertown, Massachusetts, 2014.

390 Andrienne (Goggin) Clark, Fitchburg, Massachusetts [(E-ADDRESS FOR PRIVATE USE),] to Elizabeth Banas, e-mail, 11 March 2014, "RE: Uncle John," James Clark Family File, John G. Clark, research files; privately held by Elizabeth Banas, [(E-ADDRESS & STREET ADDRESS FOR PRIVATE USE,] Belchertown, Massachusetts.

391 *Wikipedia* (http://www.wikipedia.org), "Home Owners' Loan Corporation," rev. 15: 29, 3 December 2013

392 Ibid.

393 Hampshire County, Massachusetts, Unindexed Property, Book 946: 339-340, Home Owners' Loan Corporation to John G. Clark et ux, deed, 18 January 1940, digital image; Secretary of the Commonwealth-Registry of Deeds, *Hampshire County Registry of Deeds* (http://www.masslandrecords. com : accessed 6 January 2013).

394 Andrienne (Goggin) Clark, Fitchburg, Massachusetts, to Elizabeth Banas, 18 January 2014, this account pertaining to John G. Clark was recorded by Andrienne Clark in her editorial comments regarding this book; editorial notes and commentary, privately held by Elizabeth Banas, [ADDRESS FOR PRIVATE USE,] Belchertown, Massachusetts.

395 Clark, "Growing Up In The Great Depression," n.p

396 Richer interview, 8 Mar 2014. Personal knowledge of Richer.

397 Ibid.

398 Hampshire County, Massachusetts, death certificate 37 (1972), John G. Clark; City Clerk's Office, Northampton.

399 "John G. Clark, Seven Years A Legislator," *Springfield* (MA) *Union*, 27 May 1972, p. 32, col. 3. *Courtesy of the Springfield Union.*

400 Andrienne (Goggin) Clark, Fitchburg, Massachusetts [(E-ADDRESS FOR PRIVATE USE),] to Elizabeth Banas, e-mail, 23 February 2014, "RE: Ruth," James Clark Family File, John G. Clark; privately held by Elizabeth Banas, [(E-ADDRESS) & STREET ADDRESS FOR PRIVATE USE,] Belchertown, Massachusetts.

401 "Ruth Helen Clark," *Sunday* (MA) *Republican*, 1 December 1985, p. B-23, col. 4; digital image, *GenealogyBank* (http://www.genealogybank.com: accessed 23 Feb 2014). Courtesy of the *Springfield Republican*.

402 Andrienne (Goggin) Clark, Fitchburg, Massachusetts [(E-ADDRESS FOR PRIVATE USE),] to Elizabeth Banas, e-mail, 23 February 2014, "RE: Ruth," James Clark Family File, John G. Clark; privately held by Elizabeth Banas, [(E-ADDRESS & STREET ADDRESS FOR PRIVATE USE,] Belchertown, Massachusetts. Personal knowledge of Andrienne Clark (daughter-in-law), who heard the priest who presided over Ruth's funeral tell Jack that she had converted to Catholicism.

403 Hampshire County, Massachusetts, Book 02688: 164, John P. Clark (executor) to Michael W. Kuchyt et ux, deed, 10 March 1986, digital image; Secretary of the Commonwealth-Registry of Deeds, *Hampden County Registry of Deeds* (http://www.masslandrecords.com : accessed 11 Feb 2014).

404 Cathleen Smith, daughter of Leo and Margaret (Casey) Clark ([ADDRESS FOR PRIVATE USE], Hadley, Massachusetts), interview by Elizabeth Banas, 14 February 2014, notes, privately held by Elizabeth Banas, [ADDRESS FOR PRIVATE USE,] Belchertown, Massachusetts. Cathleen noted that her father (Leo) worked at Pratt and Whitney during World War II.

405 1940 U.S. census, Hampshire County, Massachusetts, population schedule, Ward 6 Northampton, Enumeration District (ED) 8-55, sheet 4-B (penned), dwelling 96, Wilbur Cleary household; digital images, *Ancestry.com* (http://www.ancestry.com : accessed 12 Feb 2014); National Archives microfilm publication T627_1600.

406 "Cast 7-Millionth Incendiary Bomb," *Boston* (MA) *Herald*, 24 March 1945, p. 2, col. 7; digital image, *GenealogyBank* (http://www.genealogybank.com : accessed 18 Feb 2014). Courtesy of the *Boston Herald*.

407 Ibid.

408 Edward Cleary, Lorton, Virginia [(E-ADDRESS FOR PRIVATE USE),] to Elizabeth Banas, email, c. 1999, James Clark Family, Mary H. Clark; privately held by Elizabeth Banas, [(E-ADDRESS) AND STREET ADDRESS FOR PRIVATE USE,] Belchertown, Massachusetts. Edward was adopted by Mae and Wilbur at birth.

409 "U.S. World War II Army Enlistment Records 1938-1946," database, *Ancestry.com* (http://www.ancestry.com : accessed 17 Feb 2014), entry for Roger J. Cleary enlisted 23 June 1942, Massachusetts; citing "Electronic Army Serial Number Merged File, 1938-1946; World War II Army Enlistment Records; Records of the National Archives and Records Administration, Records Group 64; National Archives-College Park, College Park, Maryland.

410 Edward Cleary, "Revelations of Roger Cleary," n.p., privately held by Elizabeth Banas, Belchertown, Massachusetts. Ed Cleary forwarded this narrative to the author in February 2000 via email.

411 *The Middleton, Portland Directory* (The Price, Lee & Co., 1942), 530, entry for "Cashman, Daniel;" digital image, *Ancestry.com* (http://www.ancestry.com : accessed 13 Jan 2013); also subsequent years by the same title: (1945) 598.

412 Margaret (Cleary) Leitl, interview, 19 Mar 1999.

413 Joseph Gilboy [ADDRESS FOR PRIVATE USE,] Florence, Massachusetts, telephone interview by Elizabeth Banas, 22 Jan 2014; notes, privately held by interviewer, [ADDRESS FOR PRIVATE USE,] Belchertown, Massachusetts, 2014. Joseph Gilboy is the grandson of Julia (Cashman) Foran and John Foran. John Foran recounted this story to Joseph.

414 Margaret (Cleary) Leitl, interview, 19 Mar 1999.

415 Ibid.

416 Ibid.

417 Ed Cleary recounted this story to the author.

418 Margaret (Cleary) Leitl, interview, 19 Mar 1999.

419 Anne C. (Cleary) Goodhind, interview, c. 1999.

420 Personal knowledge of Edward Cleary. Banas, "*Mary's Garden*" n.p. There are variations of this dish, which can include meat and other vegetables.

421 Margaret (Cleary) Leitl, interview, 19 Mar 1999; Anne C. (Cleary) Goodhind, interview, 19 Mar 1999.

422 Clark, "The Clark Chronicles, 10.

423 Ibid.

424 Ibid.

425 Clark, "The Clark Chronicles," 11.

426 Northampton, Massachusetts, Hampshire County Probate District, case 25250, Jane E. McCarthy, Probate Court, Northampton; Hampshire County, "Deaths," 9: 59, for Jane E. McCarthy, City Clerk's Office, Northampton. Cause of death was noted in the register book as intestinal obstruction and colon cancer.

427 "Northampton," *Springfield (MA) Republican*, 6 November 1943, p. 7, col. 5; digital image, *GenealogyBank* (http://www.genealogybank.com : accessed 2 Sept 2013). Courtesy of the *Springfield Republican*.

428 "Mrs [.] Keefe Hears Husband 'Missing," *Springfield* (MA) *Republican*, 6 June 1946, p. 8, col. 4; digital image, *Ancestry.com* (http://www.ancestry.com : accessed 2 Mar 2014). Courtesy of the *Springfield Republican*.

429 William F. Keefe (serial no. 0920810, 1st Lieutenant Major, U.S. Army), City of Northampton roster, 1 June 1946, Records of the Adjutant General's Office, Military Records Branch, Milford, Massachusetts.

430 "Mrs Keefe [.] Hears Husband 'Missing,' *Springfield* (MA) *Republican*, 6 June 1946, p. 8. Col. 4.

431 Edward Beckett was "Mamie" Clark's husband.

432 Clark, "The Clark Chronicles," 11-12.

433 Edward Cleary, "Life at 33 Middle Street," n.p.

434 Mary Ann was the author's great-grandmother.

435 Anne (Cleary) Goodhind and Albert Goodhind were the author's parents.

436 Personal knowledge of Peg (Cleary) Leitl.

437 Ibid.

438 Ibid.

439 Andrienne (Goggin) Clark, Fitchburg, Massachusetts [(E-ADDRESS FOR PRIVATE USE),] to Elizabeth Banas, e-mail, 22 January 2014, "P.S.," James Clark Family File, John G. Clark, research files; privately held by Elizabeth Banas, [(E-ADDRESS) & STREET ADDRESS FOR PRIVATE USE,] Belchertown, Massachusetts; Jack enlisted in the Air Force for four years (5 July 1951- 4 July 1955). He was stationed in New York, Okinawa and New Mexico.

440 John G. Clark, Easthampton, Massachusetts, to Jack Clark, letter, 6 March 1955, impending death of Mary Ann Clark; Biographical and Personal, Box 1: 94, John G. Clark Collection, Special Collections and University Archives, W.E.B. Du Bois Library, University of Massachusetts, Amherst.

441 Ruth Clark, Easthampton, Massachusetts, to Jack Clark, letter, 6 March 1955, Grandmother Clark's condition; Biographical and Personal, Box 2: 41, John G. Clark Collection, Special Collections and University Archives, W.E.B. Du Bois Library, University of Massachusetts, Amherst.

442 Roger J. Cashman, Clinical Record, Death Summary, 11 March 1955, VAC Reno, Nevada, Reg. no. 15333; Pension File no. C-2286829, Veterans Administration, Boston, Massachusetts.

443 Elmer Burks (Veterans Administration Center, Reno, Nevada) to Mrs. Wilma[Wilbur] Clary [Cleary] Clark (Riverside Drive, North Hampton [Northampton], Massachusetts), letter, 9 March 1955; Pension File, Roger J. Cashman, no. C-2286829, Veterans Administration, Boston, Massachusetts.

444 Elmer Burks (Veterans Administration Center, Reno, Nevada) to Mrs. Wilma [Wilbur] Clary [Cleary] Clark (Riverside Drive, North

Hampton[Northampton], Massachusetts), telegram, 10 March 1955; Pension File, Roger J. Cashman no. C-2286829, Veterans Administration, Boston, Massachusetts.

445 Ibid.

446 Roger J. Cashman, Clinical Record, Disposition of Body, 18 March 1955, VAC Reno, Nevada, Reg. no. 15333; Pension File no. C-2286829, Veterans Administration, Boston, Massachusetts.

447 Western Union Telegraph Company to Elmer Burks (Veterans Administration Center, Reno, Nevada), notice, 15 March 1955; Pension File, Roger J. Cashman no. C-2286829, Veterans Administration, Boston Massachachusetts. Notice to Elmer Burks stating the party (D.B. Cashman) was unknown. Western Union Telegraph Company to Elmer Burks (Veterans Administration Center, Reno, Nevada), notice, 15 March 1955; Pension File, Roger J. Cashman no. C-2286829, Veterans Administration, Boston, Massachusets. Notice to Elmer Burks stating the party (Julia Faran [Foran]) was unknown.

448 John G. & Ruth Clark, Easthampton, Massachusetts, to Jack Clark, letter, 15 March 1955, The death of Mary (Cashman) Clark; Biographical and Personal, Box 2: 41, John G. Clark Collection, Special Collections and University Archives, W.E.B. Du Bois Library, University of Massachusetts, Amherst.

449 Ruth Clark, Easthampton, Massachusetts, to Jack Clark, letter, 17 March 1955, Bill, Nathalie, Nellie and Mae-funeral preparations; Biographical and Personal, Box 2: 41, John G. Clark Collection, Special Collections and University Archives, W.E.B. Du Bois Library, University of Massachusetts, Amherst.

450 Ruth Clark, Easthampton, Massachusetts, to Jack Clark, letter, 18 March 1955, Mary (Cashman) Clark's wake; Biographical and Personal, Box 2: 41,

John G. Clark Collection, Special Collections and University Archives, W.E.B. Du Bois Library, University of Massachusetts, Amherst.

451 John G, Clark, Easthampton, Massachusetts, to Jack Clark, letter, 19 March 1955, John G. Clark's observations pertaining to Mary (Cashman) Clark's wake; Biographical and Personal, Box 2: 41, John G. Clark Collection, Special Collections and University Archives, W.E.B. Du Bois Library, University of Massachusetts, Amherst.

452 Manager Reed, letter, 16 March 1955, VAC Reno, Nevada, Reg. no. 15333; Pension File no. C-2286829, Veterans Administration, Boston, Massachusetts. This letter stated that Roger Cashman's remains were to be transported to West Los Angeles on 20 March 1955. Find A Grave, Inc., *Find A Grave*, digital image (http://www.findagrave.com : accessed 16 January 2014), memorial, "Roger J. Cashman (1877-1955)," Memorial No. 3695936. Roger is interred in the Los Angeles National Cemetery (Plot 271-F2).

453 "Connecticut Death Index, 1949-2001," database, *Ancestry.com* (http://www. ancestry.com : accessed 20 January 1014), entry for Daniel B. Cashman, 08264 (1956).

454 Personal knowledge of Joseph Gilboy, [ADDRESS FOR PERSONAL USE]. Joseph Gilboy is the grandson of Julia (Cashman) Foran and John Foran. Joseph disclosed this information when I visited his home in c. 2002.

455 1870 U.S. census, Franklin Co., MA, pop. sch., Deerfield Post Office, p. 48 (penned), dwelling 318, family 385, William Conners. The entry noted that he attended school within the year. The questions pertaining to literacy were not marked, which implied he could read and write.

456 University of Iowa Labor Center, "Child Labor in U.S. History: Child Labor Reform and the U.S. Labor Movement," *Child Labor Public Education Project* (http://www.continuetolearnuiowa.edu : accessed 10 Sept 2013).

457 Ibid.

458 Ibid.

459 Hampshire Co., MA, Deeds, 499: 104.

460 *Northampton, Massachusetts, City Directory, 1885* (Northampton, MA: The Price, Lee and Co., 1885), 34, entry for "Conners, William"; digital image, *Ancestry.com* (http://www.ancestry.com : accessed 10 Sept 2103. The entry notes that William worked at Clement Manufacturing and boarded on Main Street, probably with John and Hannah.

461 1900 U.S. Census, Hampshire County, Massachusetts, population schedule, Northampton City, Enumeration District (ED) 637, sheet 5 (penned), p. 70-A (stamped), dwelling 85, family 91, Thomas Conners household; digital imagse, *Ancestry.com*, (http://www.ancestry.com : accessed 25 Aug 2011); citing National Archives microfilm publication T623; FHL microfilm 1,240,654. William was enumerated with his brother Thomas, wife Nora and their daughter (Nora) on Mill Street.

462 *Northampton, Massachusetts, City Directory, 1901* (Northampton, MA: The Price, Lee and Co., 1901), 22, entry for "Conners, William"; digital image, *Ancestry.com* (http://www.ancestry.com : accessed 10 Sept 2103. The entry notes that William was removed to Shelburne Falls.

463 Registry of Vital Records and Statistics, "Massachusetts Deaths, 1841-1915," index and images, *FamilySearch.org* (http://www.familysearch.org : accessed 10 Sept 2013), 1901, p. 53, no. 7, William Conners; FHL microfilm 2,057,733; originals held by the Massachusetts State Archives, Boston.

464 Ibid.

465 Ibid.

466 *Northampton and Easthampton Directory, 1901* (Northampton, MA: The Price Lee & Co.,) 44, "Conners, Thomas;" digital image, *Ancestry.com* (http://www.ancestry.com : accessed 12 Sept 2013); also subsequent years by the same title: (1903) 45; *Northampton City Directory,1902* (Northampton, MA: The Price Lee & Co.), 47, "Conners, Thomas"; digital image; *Ancestry. com* (http://www.ancestry.com accessed 12 Sept 2013); also subsequent years by the same title: (1906) 47, (1907) 47.

467 Myers, Helen. *Madigan Family and Myers Family*. Rep. n.p.: n.p., n.d.; photocopy held by Elizabeth Banas, Belchertown, Massachusetts.

468 Ibid. Helen Myers' report notes that Mary (McCarthy) Myers was from Killarney. The author assumes that her sister (Nora) was also born in Killarney.

469 1900 U.S. Census, Hampshire Co., MA, pop. sch., Northampton, (ED) 637, sheet 5 (penned), p. 70-A (stamped), dwell. 85, fam. 91, Thomas Conners household. This census noted that Thomas Conners and wife Nora had been married for two years.

470 Registry of Vital Records and Statistics, "Massachusetts, Births, 1841-1915," index and images, *FamilySearch* (http://www.familysearch.org : accessed 8 Aug 2013), vol. 485, p. 255, no. illegible, Nora Conners; FHL microfilm 1,843,711; originals held by the Massachusetts State Archives, Boston.

471 Registry of Vital Records and Statistics"Massachusetts, Births, 1841-1915," index and images, *FamilySearch* (http://www.familysearch.org : accessed 8 Aug 2013), vol. 543, p. 255, no. 39, James F. Conners; FHL microfilm 2,057,437; originals held by the Massachusetts State Archives, Boston.

472 "Massachusetts Registry of Vital Records and Statistics, "Massachusetts Deaths, 1841-1915," index and images, *FamilySearch* (http://www.family-search.org : accessed 6 Sept. 2013),1906, p. 189, no. 335, James Francis

Conners; FHL microfilm 004,282,913; originals held by the Massachusetts State Archives, Boston. The parents names are entered as Thomas Conners and Norah McCarthy; 25 Hinkley Street, B.S. (Bay State). Burial was at St. Mary's cemetery in Northampton, Massachusetts.

473 Registry of Vital Records and Statistics, "Massachusetts, Deaths, 1841-1915," index and images, *FamilySearch*, (http://www.familysearch.org : accessed 12 Dec 2012), 1907, p. 272, no. 313, Nora Conners; FHL micro-film 2,217,349; originals held by the Massachusetts State Archives, Boston.

474 *Wikipedia* (http://www.wikipedia.org), "Rheumatism," rev. 05:34, 11 Aug 2013.

475 1910 U.S. census, Caledonia County, Vermont, population schedule, Hardwick, Enumeration District (ED) 44, sheet 13-A (penned), p. 93 (stamped), dwelling 214, family 277, Thomas Conners; digital images, *Ancestry.com* (http://www.ancestry.com : accessed 14 Sept 2013); citing National Archives microfilm publication T624_1613; FHL microfilm 1,375,626.

476 *Northampton Directory, 1909* (Northampton, MA: The Price Lee & Co.,) 98, "Conners, Thomas;" digital image, *Ancestry.com* (http://www.ancestry.com : accessed 8 June 2015).

477 1910 U.S. census, Caledonia Co., VT, pop. sch., Hardwick, ED 44, p. 93 (stamped), dwelling 214, family 277, Thomas Conners.

478 *Wikipedia* (http://www.wikipedia.org), "Hardwick, Vermont," rev. 3:46, 24 Sept 2013. The Hardwick Hotel was the only hotel in the community.

479 1920 U.S. census, Hartford County, Connecticut, population schedule, Farmington Town, Enumeration District (ED) 41, sheet 8-B (penned), dwelling 147, family 161, Thomas Conners; digital images, *Ancestry.com*

(http://www.ancestry.com : accessed 13 Sept 2013); National Archives microfilm publication T625_181. The "number of family," includes the owner, boarders and employees. The owner is noted as James Ryan with a street address of Farmington Avenue. *Hartford Suburban Directory*, 1918-1919 (Boston, MA: Union Publishing Company, 1918), 179, entry for James B. Ryan and Cora I.; digital image, *Ancestry.com* (http://www.ancesty.com : accessed 13 Sept 2013).

480 1920 U.S. census, Hartford Co., CT, pop. sch. Farmington Town, ED 41, sheet 8-B, dwell. 147, fam. 161, Thomas Connors.

481 1920 U.S. census, Hartford Co., CT, pop. sch. Farmington Town, ED 41, sheet 8-B, dwell. 147, fam., 161, James Ryan-Charles Maxwell.

482 1920 U.S. census, Hartford Co., CT, pop. sch. Farmington Town, ED 41, sheet 8-B, dwell. 147, fam., 161, Nora Connors.

483 "Thomas F. Conners Dies, *Springfield (MA) Republican*, 16 Nov 1922, p. 8, col. 5. The paper reported that Thomas died in Cooley Dickinson Hospital. The newspaper erroneously reported that James alone was a half-brother. All of the Clark children were half-siblings to Thomas. Courtesy of the Springfield Republican. Courtesy of the Springfield Republican.

484 Northampton, Massachusetts, Deaths, 4: 221, Thomas Conners, 5 Nov 1922; City Clerk's Office, Northampton.

485 "Thomas F. Conners Dies," *Springfield (MA) Union*, 16 Nov 1922, p. 8, col. 5.

486 1930 U.S. census, Hartford County, Connecticut, population schedule, Hartford, Enumeration District (ED) 2-54, sheet 17-B (penned), n.p., dwelling 36, family 107, Nora Conners; digital images, *Ancestry.com* (http//www.

ancestry.com : accessed 15 Sept 2013); citing National Archives microfilm publication T626; FHL microfilm 2,339,999.

487 "Mrs. Nora A. Connors" [Conners], *Springfield (MA) Union*, 10 Aug 1952, p. 5, col. 3; digital images, *Ancestry.com* (http://www.ancestry.com : accessed 8 Sept 2013). The obituary was dated "Aug. 9" and stated that Nora died "today." George Myers was Thomas Conner's cousin Courtesy of the *Springfield Union*.

488 Ibid.

489 "Massachusetts Births, 1841-1915, database, *Ancestry.com* (http://www.an-cestry.com : accessed 28 Aug 2013), index entry for Anna Maria Myers, born 3 September 1859, Gill, Massachusetts. Annie (Anna) was the daughter of Ann (Wallace) Myers and Patrick Myers.

490 Registry of Vital Records and Statistics, "Massachusetts Marriages, 1841-1915," *FamilySearch* (http://ww.ancestry.com : accessed 28 Aug 2013), in-dex and images, 1904, p. 245, no. 37, Annie Myers and Michael Egan; cit-ing Northampton, Hampshire County, Massachusetts; FHL microfilm 2,057,590; originals held by the Massachusetts State Archives, Boston.

491 "Hampshire County," *Springfield* (Springfield, MA) *Republican*, 21 Apr 1904, p. 11, col. 1; digital image, *Ancestry.com* (http://www.ancestry.com : accessed 20 Aug 2013).

492 "Massachusetts Marriages, 1841-1915," *FamilySearch*, Michael F. Egan and Annie M. Myers, 1907, no. 37. The register entry notes Michael's address as 273 State Street and Annie's address as Wright Avenue. Annie's birthplace is noted as Gill.

493 Registry of Vital Records and Statistics, "Massachusetts, Deaths, 1841-1915,", *FamilySearch* (http://www.familysearch.org : accessed 10 Feb 2014),

death certificate, p. 278, (reg.) 324 (1910) Michael F. Egan; FHL microfilm 2,314,528; originals held by the Massachusetts State Archives. Michael's parents are listed as John Egan and Mary Brick.

494 Annie Egan obituary, 24 May 1934 from unidentified newspaper in Annie (Myers) Egan Scrapbook, n.d.; privately held by Helen Myers [ADDRESS FOR PRIVATE USE,] North Hatfield, Massachusetts, n.d., [Annie Egan's obituary was pasted to a page of the scrapbook.]

495 Hampshire Co., MA, death certificate no. 91(1904), Joseph Clark.

496 Ibid.

497 Ibid.

498 Ibid.

499 U.S. Social Security Administration, "Social Security Death Index," database, *GenealogyBank* (http://www.genealogybank.com : accessed 27 Aug 2013); Mary (Mae) Cleary died on 13 July 1993.

500 James Bills [ADDRESS FOR PRIVATE USE,] East Hartford, Connecticut, telephone interview by Elizabeth Banas, circa September 2013; notes, privately held by interviewer, [ADDRESS FOR PRIVATE USE,] Belchertown, Massachusetts, 2013. James Bills is the grandson of Nathalie (Coffron) Clark and William Clark.

501 St. Mary's Cemetery Office (Northampton, MA), 22 Aug 1927; citing Robert Clark, lot 96. Date entered for burial is 6 May 1938.

502 St. Mary's Cemetery Office (Northampton, MA), 22 Aug 1927.

503 Clark-Doyle Wedding (1924), handwritten notation, Annie (Myers) Egan Scrapbook. n.d., unpaginated;

504 1930 U.S. census, Hampshire County, Massachusetts, population schedule, Northampton, Enumeration District (ED) 8-31, sheet 5-B (penned), dwelling 96, family 135, John P. McCarthy; digital image, *Ancestry.com* (http://www.ancestry.com : accessed 23 Jan 2014); citing National Archives microfilm publication T626; FHL microfilm 2,340,647.

505 1910 U.S. census, Franklin County, Massachusetts, population schedule, Montague, Enumeration District (ED) 507, sheet 1-A (penned), p. 28 (stamped), dwelling 3, family 8, Jennie Doyle; digital image, *Ancestry.com* (http://www.ancestry.com : accessed 27 Dec 2011); citing National Arcives microfilm publication T624_589; FHL microfilm 1,374,602.

506 1920 U.S. census, Hampshire County, Massachusetts, population schedule, Northampton, Enumeration Distict (ED) 174, sheet 8-A (penned), p. 181 (stamped), dwelling 155, family 151, Nicholas Doyle household, digital image; *Ancestry.com* (http://www.ancestry.com : accessed 9 May 2014); National Archives microfilm publication T625_705.

507 "Napoleon Campbell Dead," *Springfield (*Springfield, MA*) Republican*, 24 April 1926, p.4, col. 5; digital image, *GenealogyBank* (http://www.genealogy-bank.com : accessed 26 Dec 2011). Courtesy of the *Springfield Republican*.

508 Ibid.

509 Notation and date of Mary Purcell's marriage to Napoleon Campbell (6 Jan 1913) in Annie (Myers) Egan, "scrapbook,"n.d., privately held by Helen Myers [ADDRESS FOR PRIVATE USE,] North Hatfield, Massachusetts.

510 "1930 United States Federal Census," database, *Ancestry.com* (http://www.ancestry.com : accessed 24 Jan 2014), entry for Napoleon Campbell born c. 1877, Pittsfield, Berkshire, Massachusetts.

Index

Author Biography

 Elizabeth Anne Banas is genealogist and writer. She specializes in research in Hampden, Hampshire, Franklin and Berkshire Counties in Massachusetts. She also offers research services in Hartford County, Connecticut. You can learn more about her by visiting E.A. Banas Genealogy Services (http://www.eabanasgenealogyservices.com). Elizabeth resides in the quaint community of Belchertown, Massachusetts with her husband George H. Banas. She is a member of the National Association for Professional Genealogists, The New England Association for Professional Genealogists and the National Genealogical Society.

Made in the USA
Middletown, DE
31 July 2015